WAR
in
HEAVEN

Other Books by Derek Prince

EXPANDED EDITION

WAR
in
HEAVEN

TAKING YOUR PLACE
IN THE EPIC BATTLE WITH EVIL

DEREK PRINCE

Chosen
a division of Baker Publishing Group
Minneapolis, Minnesota

© 2003, 2015 by Derek Prince Ministries International

Published by Chosen Books
11400 Hampshire Avenue South
Bloomington, Minnesota 55438
www.chosenbooks.com

Chosen Books is a division of
Baker Publishing Group, Grand Rapids, Michigan

Printed in the United States of America

Library of Congress Cataloging-in-Publication Data
Prince, Derek, author.
    War in heaven : taking your place in the epic battle with evil / Derek
Prince.— Revised edition.
        pages cm
    Includes index.
    Summary: "This revised bestseller provides answers to the fundamental questions of evil and reveals why spiritual warfare is such an important part of God's plan for each of us"— Provided by publisher.
    ISBN 978-0-8007-9548-1 (pbk. : alk. paper)
    1. Conversion—Christianity. 2. Economy of God. 3. Devil. I. Title.
    BV4921.3.P75 2015
    231'.5—dc23   2014041708

Cover design by Dual Identity

For more than two years, while working on this book, I have experienced an ongoing battle against many forms of sickness and infirmity. Some of the enemies I have encountered have been two forms of cancer, polymyalgia rheumatica, double pneumonia, congestive heart failure, eye surgery, two hours of surgery on my scalp, a gallstone attack.

At one point in time, I was delirious for more than a week due to an infection. Twice I had the experience of going to bed in one place and waking up in a hospital bed in another place.

Through all this, I have been continuously upheld by the love and the prayers of thousands of Christians in many parts of the globe. I never knew there was so much love available to me!

To all you who have prayed, I now gratefully dedicate this book.

> But thanks be to God,
> who gives us the victory
> through our Lord Jesus Christ.
> 1 Corinthians 15:57

Contents

Contents

Foreword

Derek Prince lived on a wartime footing. Most of his Christian experience took place in a context of intense physical and spiritual warfare. As believers in Jesus Christ in these present challenging days, we would do well to take note of the example he set and the lessons he conveys in this book.

Derek came to faith in Jesus Christ while in the British army in World War II. That was his beginning point—preparing for battle. As a soldier, he was surrounded by the conflict in North Africa—integrally involved in the battle of El Alamein, a turning point in that world war.

Shortly after the war's end while living in Jerusalem, Derek, his wife Lydia and their entire family were eyewitnesses to the massive outbreak of fighting surrounding the birth of Israel in 1948. Shells and shrapnel filled the living area of their home in Jerusalem—the home from which they eventually fled.

During the late 1950s, a time when Derek was director of a mission school in Kenya, warfare in adjacent nations that were battling communist insurgencies encroached upon their lives as well. Soon after his time in Africa, returning to Great Britain, then to Canada, and then to the United States, God led Derek directly into a ministry that included one distinct and unique aspect—deliverance and spiritual warfare.

Is it any wonder, then, that Derek could speak so authoritatively in *War in Heaven* on the topic of the battles we wage in earthly and heavenly realms?

You are holding in your hands a rather controversial book. What makes it controversial? At least two things:

First, some Christians refuse to accept the reality that believers are in a war that we are required to fight. Far too many deny the need to take up not only defensive but also offensive spiritual weapons to deal with the enemies opposing us. Huge numbers of believers are not even aware of the battle swirling around them—one into which they will inevitably be swept as participants, either willingly or unwillingly.

The second cause of controversy revolves around some of the theories Derek Prince presents regarding the origin and nature of the spiritual enemies facing us.

There are probably other areas of controversy as well—because this is an unsettling book by an uncommon warrior.

How should you approach this publication, filled as it is with the potential for controversy and upset? Our suggestion is that you simply read what Derek has presented in *War in Heaven* and then decide for yourself.

Supernatural warfare is going on all around us, and it demands our undivided attention. Forewarned is forearmed. If you possess a strong desire to prepare yourself more fully for battle and victory as a soldier in the Kingdom of God, we invite you to read on!

The International Publishing Team
of Derek Prince Ministries

Preface

I t is obvious that life is full of conflict and war. Why is this so? Does Scripture give us any explanation for the cause?

Although the Bible tells us everything we need to know for our spiritual benefit, it leaves many questions open to interpretation. On some of the issues we will discuss in this book, issues on which scholars have advanced numerous interpretations, Scripture does not provide us with sufficient evidence to speak with certainty.

The answers and impressions I bring you are the result of study, meditation, prayer and practical experience. I certainly do not claim to have answered all the questions that arise. There is no limit to such questions! But we should never allow the things we do not understand to obscure for us the areas of truth in which God has provided clear understanding.

What we know for certain is that, confronted with the rebellion of Adam and Eve, God set in motion a secret plan conceived in eternity. Historically this plan was unfolded in the life, death and resurrection of Jesus Christ. Through what He accomplished on the cross, we are enabled to have a special relationship with God.

All heaven is waiting for the full manifestation of His victory.

1   What Is Your Picture of Heaven?

What is your view of heaven? Do you believe that there is such a place? If so, is it a place of ethereal light and music with choirs worshiping God in settings of awe-inspiring beauty and elaborate architecture? Do you envisage dazzling displays of gold and silver with an array of innumerable precious stones? Doubtless this is true in a measure, but it is not the complete picture.

Perhaps you see heaven as the inner surface of a vast, concave dome that stretches out over the whole earth. As the edge of the dome approaches the horizon, it sometimes gives the impression that it will fall short. But it never does! It always covers the earth beneath it.

Almost all of earth's inhabitants have some impression of heaven. As we contemplate the vast possibilities, we need to bear in mind that various terms are used to describe heaven. There is the single noun, *heaven,* which emphasizes its overall unity; other expressions apparently refer to its different aspects or parts. For instance, the terms *heavenlies* or *heavenly places* suggest a number of different locations all combined under the heading *heaven*. These places may be given over at various times to different beings and different activities.

In 2 Corinthians 12:2–4 Paul writes:

> I know a man in Christ who fourteen years ago—whether in the body I do not know, or whether out of the body I do not know, God knows—such a one was caught up to the third heaven. And I know such a man—whether in the body or out of the body I do not know, God knows—how he was caught up into Paradise and heard inexpressible words, which it is not lawful [or not possible] for a man to utter.

This passage indicates that there are altogether three heavens, one immediately above the other. The topmost is what Paul describes as the "third heaven." It is the location of Paradise and the place of God's personal dwelling, the most sacred place in the universe. It is passages such as this one that give us the concept often associated with heaven—purity or holiness. The words spoken there are so sacred that they may not be repeated outside.

Almost all of earth's inhabitants have some impression of heaven.

Paradeisos (paradise) is the Greek word for a "garden." It describes God's garden in heaven. Paradise is the ultimate destination of all sinners who

16

have truly repented and who have persevered in the life of faith. On the cross, Jesus promised the penitent thief that the two of them would be together that day in Paradise: "And Jesus said to him, 'Assuredly, I say to you, today you will be with Me in *Paradise*'" (Luke 23:43, emphasis added).

The book of Revelation introduces us to an area referred to as the "mid-heaven" or "the midst of heaven." To my understanding, this describes some kind of large expanse with different types of beings coming and going. The following verses describe various powerful beings who make proclamations from the mid-heaven.

> And I looked, and I heard an angel flying through the midst of heaven [literally, *mid-heaven*], saying with a loud voice, "Woe, woe, woe to the inhabitants of the earth, because of the remaining blasts of the trumpet of the three angels who are about to sound!"
>
> 8:13

> Then I saw another angel flying in the midst of heaven [literally, *mid-heaven*], having the everlasting gospel to preach to those who dwell on the earth—to every nation, tribe, tongue, and people.
>
> 14:6

> Then I saw an angel standing in the sun; and he cried with a loud voice, saying to all the birds that fly in the midst of heaven [literally, *mid-heaven*], "Come and gather together for the supper of the great God."
>
> 19:17

The Greek word used for the mid-heaven is *mesouranema,* which means precisely that, the mid-heaven. This could be the second heaven.

We might assume, finally, that the visible heaven—the heaven that is visible to our natural eyesight—is the first heaven. All earth's inhabitants are familiar to some degree with this heaven.

What about the denizens of heaven? What kind of creatures are they? The name most commonly given to them is *angels.* The word *angel* is derived from the Greek noun *angelos,* which is the standard word for "messenger." Angels, therefore, are viewed as messengers sent from heaven.

Not all angels, however, are messengers. They have various other potential functions. Whatever their tasks, they are sent forth by God for His purposes. But Scripture makes it clear that there are also evil angels sent forth by Satan for his purposes. At times, opposition or conflicts may occur between the angels of God and the angels of Satan. Some of these conflicts are depicted in Scripture, particularly in the book of Daniel.

We are thus confronted by the inescapable fact that our world as we know it today is a scene of conflict. Furthermore, this conflict is not restricted to earth. It is also a vital factor in all that takes place in heaven.

The angels sent forth by God have three main tasks. First, as already stated, they are God's messengers. Secondly, they are God's agents sent forth to protect those who may be in danger. These are normally described as "guardian angels." In Matthew 18:10 Jesus speaks about children who have angels in heaven who continually see the face of the Father. By implication, the Father's watchful eye directs those angels to potentially vulnerable children. In the third category are warrior angels who are engaged in conflict with opposing angels.

Many Christians assume that heaven is a place of unbroken peace and harmony, beauty and worship. This may well be true of the third heaven, but it does not apply to the first and second heavens. Some Scriptures paint a very different picture of what is currently going on in the second heaven. As already stated, it is at times the scene of great conflict between warring angels—some serving God and others serving Satan. It is primarily in the heavenly regions that such conflict takes place.

> Many Christians assume that heaven is a place of unbroken peace and harmony, beauty and worship.

It is here, too, that Satan pours out a stream of slanderous accusations against the Christians on earth who are serving the Lord. In Revelation 12:10, he is described by an angel as the "accuser of our brethren, who accused them before our God day and night."

This Scripture goes on to predict that Satan will be cast down from heaven. But until this happens, it is clear that he still continues to occupy a place somewhere in the heavenlies and that he is filling the air with malicious accusations against God's people.

A verse that follows is a warning to earth's inhabitants as to what they may expect when the devil is ultimately cast down from heaven to earth: "Woe to the inhabitants of the earth and the sea! For the devil has come down to you, having great wrath, because he knows that he has a short time" (Revelation 12:12).

> Many Christians habitually speak as if Satan were confined in hell, but this is not true.

These verses look forward to a period when Satan has but "a short time." They may well be close at hand, but they have not yet been fulfilled. Certainly the events described have not been fulfilled by anything that has happened in heaven up to this time.

We need, therefore, to be realistic about Satan's current activities. Many Christians habitually speak as if Satan were confined in hell, but this is not true. There are two satanic princes called Death and Hades that rule in hell (see Revelation 20:13), but Satan himself roams freely throughout the universe. This is plainly depicted in Job 1:6–7:

> Now there was a day when the sons of God [i.e., the angels] came to present themselves before the LORD, and Satan also came among them. And the LORD said to Satan, "From where do you come?" So Satan answered the LORD and said, "From going to and fro on the earth, and from walking back and forth on it."

This passage indicates that Satan may even come before God's presence in company with righteous angels who are serving the Lord. It seems, however, that in this instance the Lord was the only one who actually identified him as Satan. The other angels did not recognize who he was. This would agree with Paul's statement in 2 Corinthians 11:14: "For Satan himself transforms himself into an angel of light."

In the next chapter we will begin to analyze how this conflict in the heavenlies affects our daily lives.

Questions for This Study

1. How many heavens are there and how is each described?

    (a) _____

    (b) _____

    (c) _____

2. Who are the creatures flying in the second heaven, and what is the standard word derived from the Greek?

    _____ and _____

3. The conflict between the angels of God and the angels of Satan is not restricted to _____ but is also in _____.

4. What are the three main tasks of angels sent forth by God?

    (a) _____

    (b) _____

    (c) _____

Life Application

1. How has this chapter affected your thinking about heaven and angels?

2. Why is it important to see conflicts from a spiritual as well as a natural point of view?

Notes

_____

_____

_____

_____

_____

_____

Memory Verse

Are they not all ministering spirits sent forth to minister for those who will inherit salvation?

Hebrews 1:14

Faith Response

Father, I approach this study to learn more about the unseen world around me. Open the eyes of my understanding to hear and see what You have to teach me concerning spiritual conflict. Show me what my part is. Thank You, Lord.

2   **Life Is a Battle!**

One thing that becomes glaringly apparent early on for most of us is that life is full of conflict, struggle and war. Many of us simply accept this as fact without raising any questions. Some years ago, however, I began to meditate on this and I asked myself, *What is the reason for all the conflict in our world? Have we accepted as normal something that is abnormal? Why are there wars? Why are there struggles, strife and disputes? Does Scripture give us any clear explanation of a real cause for all this conflict? Did it have a beginning and will it always be so?*

These are questions I have turned over in my own mind for many years. What I bring you in this book will be the fruit of much meditation, prayer and study and also of practical experience.

When we look at the New Testament, we find that conflict, war and embracing the attitude of a "spiritual soldier" are all accepted as a normal part of Christian living. This conflict is not something exceptional that a few Christians may encounter. The Bible teaches that all Christians must be prepared to encounter conflict and warfare in the spiritual realm.

First, we will look at several Scriptures that depict conflict and warfare as a normal part of Christian living. Then we will search the Scriptures to see how it all began.

The Christian Soldier

Our first reference is 2 Corinthians 10:3–5:

> For though we live in the world, we do not wage war as the world does. The weapons we fight with are not the weapons of the world. On the contrary, they have divine power to demolish strongholds. We demolish arguments and every pretension that sets itself up against the knowledge of God, and we take captive every thought to make it obedient to Christ.
>
> NIV

Paul is speaking here of *all* Christians. He says we wage war—not in the fleshly realm but in the spiritual realm.

We have weapons for our warfare, and we are attacking and demolishing strongholds. Thus, Paul uses four military expressions in these three verses: *war, weapons, demolishing strongholds, taking captives*. These are an essential and inevitable part of the Christian life.

Notice from the start that the New Testament does not place Christians on the defensive but on the *offensive*. This is one of the biggest mistakes of contemporary Christendom: We view ourselves as being on the defensive. Take, for instance, the well-known book by Jesse Penn-Lewis entitled *War on the Saints*. The very title assumes that the initiative is taken by our enemy. This is an error. *It is we Christians who should be making war on our enemy.* We should not be waiting to see what the enemy will do to us.

> The Bible teaches that all Christians must be prepared to encounter conflict and warfare in the spiritual realm.

In Matthew 16:18, Jesus makes a promise concerning His Church: "On this rock I will build My church, and the gates of Hades shall not prevail against it."

In the warfare of those days, the "gate" of a city was the place of weakness on which an invading army would focus its main attacks. Jesus is therefore promising us that we (the Church) will be taking the offensive against satanic strongholds and penetrating their gates and that they will not be able to keep us out. It is we who should be keeping the enemy in an attitude of suspense: "What are these Christians going to do to me next!" Part of the ultimate purpose of this book is to restore the initiative to God's people.

In 1 Timothy 1:18 we find words spoken by Paul to Timothy as a minister of the Gospel: "This charge I commit to you, son Timothy, according to the prophecies previously made concerning you, that by them you may wage the good warfare."

Timothy was a young man who had been called early in life to the ministry of the Gospel. Prophecies had been given over him outlining the type of ministry to which God was calling him. These warned him of conflict, opposition and even danger. Paul is saying, "I want you to remember these prophecies that you have received, and in the light of them to wage good warfare. You must serve wholeheartedly, with courage and dedication in the spiritual warfare that is a direct result of your commitment to serve Jesus Christ." Again, we see the word *warfare*.

In 2 Timothy 2:3–4 Paul returns to the same theme, applying the word *soldier* to Timothy to describe his Christian service.

> You therefore must endure hardship as a good soldier of Jesus Christ. No one engaged in warfare entangles himself with the affairs of this life, that he may please him who enlisted him as a soldier.

Paul assumes that Timothy is a soldier, engaged in spiritual warfare, chosen for this warfare by the Lord Jesus Christ. He must, therefore, conduct himself in a way that is appropriate to his position as a soldier. Having served as a soldier five and a half years in the British Army, I know what a soldier's life is like. It is entirely different from the life of a civilian. A soldier has to recognize the fact that he cannot live like a civilian! Paul is bringing home this lesson to Timothy as a minister of the Gospel: "You cannot live like other people. You have a special calling. You have special responsibilities. You are set apart, just as a soldier is set apart to a special way of life." Again we notice the assumption that the Christian life involves warfare.

Turning to Ephesians 6:12, we find another vivid picture of the Christian life:

> For we do not wrestle against flesh and blood, but against principalities, against powers, against the rulers of the darkness of this age, against spiritual hosts of wickedness in the heavenly places.

Paul here illustrates the Christian life by a metaphor from the Olympic Games: the wrestling match. He says that as Christians we are involved in a wrestling match. Wrestling involves the entire person. It is the most total bodily form of conflict in sport. This is the particular type of contest that Paul uses to illustrate the Christian life.

Allow me to give you a more literal rendering of this verse: "For our wrestling match is not against flesh and blood—we are not wrestling against mere human personalities—but against principalities (or rulerships), against authorities, against the world dominators of this present darkness, against spirits of wickedness in the heavenlies."

These statements prompt many questions. As this book unfolds, we will seek to deal with them. But notice what a remarkable picture confronts us: Christians involved in a wrestling match, not against human persons but against spiritual beings, not limited to the earth but extending also to the heavenlies.

The Christian life is not just sweetness and harp music; every committed Christian will find warfare to be part of his total experience. Because our government in heaven is at war, we on earth are automatically at war also.

Let me illustrate this by an example from personal experience. In 1939, I was a British citizen resident in Britain. On the third of September, the British government officially declared war on Nazi Germany. Because my government had legally declared war, I was automatically involved. I did not have to make an individual personal decision. I was at war with Germany. If I refused to accept that, I would have been delinquent in my obligations as a British citizen. I did not have a choice to make. It had been made for me.

> The Christian life is not just sweetness and harp music; every committed Christian will find warfare to be part of his total experience.

I was, however, given the freedom to choose a branch of the forces in which I would serve. I volunteered for noncombatant medical duties. As a result, I spent five and a half years in Britain's Royal Army Medical Corps.

The same principle applies in the spiritual realm. Our heavenly government is at war with the kingdom of Satan. Therefore, we are required to take our places as soldiers in this war. As in my own case, we may be given freedom to choose the field of service, but we cannot opt out of the war.

This truth about spiritual warfare is enforced by the way the Bible speaks about God Himself as a military commander. This language does not occur just once or twice but is found throughout Scripture. For example, Exodus

15:3 records a song that Moses and the children of Israel sang after passing through the waters of the Red Sea. Seeing God's judgment in the annihilation of the entire Egyptian army, the Israelites give expression to their gratitude and to their sense of triumph and victory in this song: "The Lord is a man of war; the Lord is His name."

In the original Hebrew, the word Lord, when capitalized, represents the sacred name of four letters rendered "Jehovah" or "Yahweh." Modern scholars tend to use "Yahweh." So we might render that verse: "The Lord is a man of war; Yahweh is His name." The verse that follows reads: "Pharaoh's chariots and his army He has cast into the sea; his chosen captains also are drowned in the Red Sea" (verse 4).

Notice that God, as a military commander, has brought total defeat upon the enemies of His people. It is not just a metaphor but actually expresses the results achieved.

Then in Joshua 5 we see Jericho besieged by the armies of Israel. Joshua is no doubt seeking to plan his strategy to capture this very well-defended and highly fortified ancient city. A man appears to Joshua who is indeed no ordinary man, but rather the "Lord" Himself. This is illustrated in the following three verses:

> And it came to pass, when Joshua was by Jericho, that he lifted his eyes and looked, and behold, a Man stood opposite him with His sword drawn in His hand. And Joshua went to Him and said to Him, "Are You for us or for our adversaries?" So He said, "No, but as Commander of the army of the Lord I have now come." And Joshua fell on his face to the earth and worshiped, and said to

Him, "What does my Lord say to His servant?" Then the Commander of the Lord's army said to Joshua, "Take your sandal off your foot, for the place where you stand is holy." And Joshua did so.

Joshua 5:13–15

Here is a divine Person coming to Joshua—with His sword drawn—who reveals His identity: "I am the captain of the army of the Lord." There is no question in my mind that this is the One who was later manifested in human history as Jesus of Nazareth, the eternal Son of God. This Commander was not the Father but the Son.

This is one of many Old Testament Scriptures in which He was manifested to human beings, including Abraham, Jacob, Moses and Joshua. The "Lord" declared Himself to be a military commander and He had a drawn sword in His hand! This is part of the Bible's total picture of God.

A similar presentation of the Lord as a warrior occurs in Psalm 24:8: "Who is this King of glory? The Lord strong and mighty, the Lord mighty in battle."

Those words are so vivid for me because in World War II, I served with the British Eighth Army in the North African desert. Our forces suffered a series of reverses, and, in fact, I took part in the longest retreat recorded in the history of the British Army: about seven hundred miles of continuous retreating! We got to the very gates of Cairo, to a place called El Alamein, and then the British government, under Winston Churchill, appointed a new commander, whose name was Montgomery. We certainly needed a new commander, because the discipline, the morale and the efficiency of the British forces were in a shocking condition.

As a new Christian, I had been praying this prayer: "Lord, give us a leader such that it will be for Your glory to give us victory through him!" Then the Battle of El Alamein was fought and won—the first real Allied victory in the war, and a major turning point.

About two days after the battle, I was in the desert with a small portable radio on the tailgate of my truck. I was listening as the news commentator gave an account of the preparations for the Battle of El Alamein as he had witnessed them at the British headquarters. He described how General Montgomery—then an unknown figure—had called his officers and men together before the battle was joined, and said in public, "Let us ask the Lord, mighty in battle, to give us the victory." It was as though God spoke to me at that moment and said, *That is the answer to your prayer!* Montgomery's words were taken from Psalm 24:8, already quoted: "Who is this King of glory? The LORD strong and mighty, the LORD mighty in battle."

The Bible emphasizes continually that the Lord is a man of war! In agreement with this, we find more than a hundred passages in Scripture where Jehovah is called the "LORD of hosts" or the "God of hosts." Remember that the word *host* is the old English term for "army." He is the God of armies, the "LORD of armies."

Isaiah 13:4 uses this word, for instance, in declaring a prophecy of God's judgment on the city of Babylon. Historically, Babylon was captured by armies and destroyed. Before all this took place, however, Isaiah was granted a vision of God's judgment on Babylon, and he paints a vivid picture of a great company of nations gathering together against this city:

The noise of a multitude in the mountains, like that of many people! A tumultuous noise of the kingdoms of nations gathered together! The LORD of hosts [*tsava*] musters the army for battle.

The Hebrew word used here for *hosts, tsava,* is the modern Hebrew word for the army of Israel. The word has never changed its meaning. God is still the "LORD of armies" today and He can—and does—still muster His forces for battle.

How War Began

For many years, I have pondered the background of the conflict in our world. What is the root cause of the warfare and unrest on every hand? Who are the opposing forces involved? We have seen that God is a military commander, and we are part of an army under His command. But what—and whom—is He fighting against?

Let me seek to answer the first question. The background—the root cause—of all unrest, conflict and war can be summed up in a single word: *rebellion.* This is the root problem of the universe: rebellion against the righteous government of God. Our world today is full of rebels.

We might think of it like this. Human problems can be depicted by the three main parts of a tree: branches, trunk and roots. I find that most people are preoccupied with the branches. If you are hoping to remove a tree, but just cut off a few branches, you have not really changed things very much. It is the trunk that carries the branches and the roots that feed the trunk.

Consider the woman who becomes an alcoholic. The addiction to alcohol is just the symptom or branch. We need to get below that to the trunk and the roots—that is, her attitude and her relationship to her husband. Perhaps he has been unfaithful, spends the money in a way she does not approve of and emotionally abuses the children. The bitterness and resentment she has built up against her husband are the trunk and roots. We will never solve her problem by merely dealing with her alcoholism. We must deal with her attitude and relationship toward her husband. Is she willing to forgive him and receive him? If not, even if she gets rid of alcoholism, it will be followed by another addiction or similar problem.

The Church in general is grappling most of the time with branches. It does not normally get below that level and deal with the trunk, much less the roots. We must dig down to the *root problem*, and the root problem is rebellion.

In introducing to humanity the message of Jesus and the Gospel, John the Baptist makes a definitive statement: "And even now the ax is laid to the *root* of the trees. Therefore every tree which does not bear good fruit is cut down and thrown into the fire" (Matthew 3:10, emphasis added).

The message of the Gospel is *radical*; that is, it deals with the root. God is saying, in effect, "I am no longer content with merely cutting off the branches or even cutting down the trunk. I am dealing with the root, which is the will set in independence from Me." Independence in its turn inevitably becomes defiance.

Most contemporary presentations of the Gospel do not go deep enough. They do not deal with the sin of rebellion against God. We would be surprised to discover how many good church members all around us have never made a true submission to God.

Look at the Lord's Prayer, a very familiar passage of Scripture. Notice the opening phrases of this pattern prayer found in Matthew 6:9–13:

"In this manner, therefore, pray: Our Father in heaven, hallowed be Your name. Your kingdom come. Your will be done on earth as it is in heaven. Give us this day our daily bread. And forgive us our debts, as we forgive our debtors. And do not lead us into temptation, but deliver us from the evil one. For Yours is the kingdom and the power and the glory forever. Amen."

The opening phrases define the whole attitude and atmosphere of this prayer. First of all, we pray as members of one Body. We do not pray "my" Father, we pray "our" Father. There are other people besides ourselves involved in this relationship with God. One of the greatest problems people have is thinking that no one else has suffered what they are suffering! I hear it all the time: "Nobody else has ever suffered like this, Brother Prince. You don't know what I have gone through!" So many people have told me exactly the same thing!

The Bible teaches us to regard ourselves as members together of one Body. The word *our* is very important: "Our Father." We are reminded that we are sons and daughters of God. We have the right to come to Him as a Father, but we must not forget that we have brothers and sisters in our heavenly family.

Then we have to learn reverence and respect: "Hallowed be Your name." Few sections of the church today have genuine reverence for God. We may demand an outward conformity of behavior, but that is very different from honoring, respecting and fearing Almighty God. "Hallowed be Your name."

The next phrase is "Your kingdom come." God has a Kingdom and His ultimate purpose in this dispensation is to bring His Kingdom into being on earth. When I say, "Your kingdom come," I am lining myself up with God's purposes. It is not just a nice religious phrase. I am saying, "God, may Your Kingdom come—and here I am, ready to play my part in the coming of Your Kingdom." That is why I am saying it. I am identifying myself with the purpose of God.

> One of the greatest problems people have is thinking that no one else has suffered what they are suffering!

Then I say, "Your will be done on earth as it is in heaven." How is God's will done in heaven? As I understand it, it is done perfectly. There are no hitches, no frustrations and no delays. God's will goes through perfectly in heaven. Jesus taught us to pray that it should go the same way on earth. If Jesus taught us to pray that, then I believe it is a possibility. I do not believe that Jesus would teach us to pray for something absolutely impossible. But when I pray "Your will be done on earth," you know where it has to begin? With me! I have to submit myself without reservation to the will of God.

I think of the conversion of Charles Finney. He was one of the greatest preachers that the Church has ever known

and a man with an outstanding ministry of bringing sinners to conviction and conversion. One of the remarkable
facts about Finney's ministry as an evangelist is that over
two-thirds of his converts maintained their stand as Christians. In contrast, it is estimated that only approximately
one-third of D. L. Moody's converts remained Christians.
There was something in the ministry of Finney that produced gripping conviction, and I believe it goes back to
Finney's own conversion.

Finney was a respectable lawyer when somebody confronted him with the Gospel and his need for salvation.
He turned it over in his mind and thought, *Well, if there
is such a thing as salvation, I probably need to be saved.
It would be a good thing to be saved.*

Because he was a respectable lawyer, however, he did
not think that it would be dignified to be saved in public,
so he decided to go out into the woods.

Off he went to the woods to pray. Then he asked himself, *Well, what am I going to pray? The Lord's Prayer,
that is a good prayer. There is nothing wrong with praying that.*

So he started out, "Our Father, which art in heaven, hallowed be Thy name. Thy kingdom come. . . ." As he got
ready to say the next phrase, "Thy will be done on earth,"
it dawned on him that this involved him. He could not
say "Thy will be done on earth" unless he was prepared
without reservation to submit to God's will in his own life.
Otherwise, he would be a hypocrite.

At that point, the Holy Spirit moved in and through that
phrase—*Thy will be done*—showed Finney what a rebel
he really was: a polite, respectable, law-abiding, religious

rebel. God dealt with him powerfully, breaking him down into a state of total submission.

Shortly afterward God baptized him in the Holy Spirit. There is no question about what happened to Finney. He said, "I received a mighty baptism of the Holy Spirit," and then he continued, "I literally bellowed out the unutterable gushings of my soul." He gave forth an utterance in what we would call today an unknown tongue. Here is the real secret: first of all, the deep conviction, and secondly, a mighty anointing of the Holy Spirit.

Returning to our text, "Your will be done," we find that it means, "Lord, I am not going to be a rebel any longer." Yet many people who regularly say the Lord's Prayer have never realized to what they are committing themselves. I have found that people will never have a deep, settled, permanent inward peace until they make a total submission to Almighty God. This is the message of Isaiah 57:19–21: "'I create the fruit of the lips: Peace, peace to him who is far off and to him who is near,' says the LORD, 'and I will heal him'" (verse 19).

God is offering peace and healing to all men. *To him who is far off* is usually a form of speech for the Gentiles. *To him who is near* refers to Israel. God is offering peace and healing to all people, but some can never receive peace because they will never lay down their arms of rebellion. Therefore, God goes on to say: "But the wicked are like the troubled sea, when it cannot rest, whose waters cast up mire and dirt. 'There is no peace,' says my God, 'for the wicked'" (verses 20–21).

As long as we retain that attitude of rebellion, we cannot rest. We are like the waves of the sea, continually rolling and breaking, casting up the mire and the dirt at its edge. Watch the sea! It cannot rest! Look again at these words: "The wicked [the rebellious] are like the troubled sea, when it cannot rest. . . . 'There is no peace . . . for the wicked.'" The most convincing evidence that you are living a righteous life is that you have deep, settled, abiding inward peace. Few people today are truly at rest.

> God is offering peace and healing to all men.

I was ministering in New Zealand with some Baptist friends who were talking about their college-age Sunday school class. They described how a young woman who was a trained nurse came into the class. She did not profess to be a Christian but wanted to study the Bible. One day this young woman challenged the teacher about the joy and peace that are the fruit of the Holy Spirit. She said, "I will believe that when I am not continually giving sedation and tranquilizers to the members of your church that I have to visit in their homes! If you have joy and peace, why all the sedation? Why all the tranquilizers? It doesn't go together!"

That is the truth! That is why I say that few people in our contemporary society have real, deep, settled inward peace. Why? Because we are a world of rebels! Many times we are religious rebels, but rebels just the same. I believe that a confrontation is coming, a showdown between God and the people of the Western culture. I envisage this in my spirit, and I praise God for it. The real issue will be this: total submission! *If Almighty God is willing to come into my life, there is only one logical place I can offer Him:*

total supremacy, complete Lordship. Anything short of that is a sham.

We find ourselves confronted with this fact of rebellion: rebellion inside us, rebellion in the world around us, rebellion against government, rebellion against God, rebellion in children against parents, rebellion in students against teachers and so on. Everywhere we see rebellion burgeoning and increasing. When did rebellion begin? Who was the first rebel?

Questions for This Study

1. What three actions are accepted in the New Testament as a normal part of Christian living?

   (a) _____

   (b) _____

   (c) _____

2. Why must a soldier recognize the fact that he cannot live like a civilian?

   _____

   _____

3. The message of the Gospel is _____; it deals with the _____ _____. The will set in _____ from God inevitably becomes

   _____.

4. What is the most convincing evidence that you are living a righteous life?

   _____

Life Application

1. How do you view your calling and commitment to the Lord and His Church as a soldier called by God?

2. How many weapons of spiritual warfare can you think of, and how can each be effective in helping you win your battles?

Notes

_____

_____

_____

_____

_____

_____

_____

_____

Memory Verse

You therefore must endure hardship as a good soldier of Jesus Christ. No one engaged in warfare entangles himself with the affairs of this life, that he may please him who enlisted him as a soldier.

2 Timothy 2:3–4

Faith Response

Father, I do see that You have called me as a soldier in this war. I willingly submit myself to You and say, Your Kingdom come, Your will be done in my life in every way. Teach me and train me to walk in my calling faithfully. Reveal to me as a soldier what my place is and what You have for me to do.

3   A Pre-Adamic World

Scholars have advanced numerous interpretations regarding the possible existence of a pre-Adamic race. Nonetheless Scripture does not provide us with sufficient evidence to speak with certainty. The answers and impressions I bring you are the result of study, meditation, prayer and practical experience. I certainly do not claim to have answered all the questions that arise, and it is important that we never allow the things we do not fully understand to obscure for us the areas of truth in which God has provided clear understanding.

As I mentioned in the preface of this book, there are certain issues that surface through the study of Scripture that raise many questions. After decades of meditation on the first few verses of the Book of Genesis, I have come to the conclusion that God's judgment against rebellion could have taken place prior to any of the six days of creation as depicted in Genesis. In Genesis 1:2 we are told that the earth was "without form and void" (in Hebrew, *tohu va bohu*). My examination of other passages where this phrase is used suggests that it always describes the effect of some judgmental act on the part of God. This would indicate that the first of God's judgments took place between Genesis 1:1 and Genesis 1:2. Possibly it could have been a judgment on the original rebellion of Lucifer (Satan). It is outside the scope of this book to analyze all this in detail. I believe, however, that this is an area that can give us insight when we are conducting intercession and spiritual warfare.

Contrary to many people's thinking, rebellion did not begin on earth but in heaven. It did not begin with a human being but with an archangel who has come to be known as Satan, although his original name was Lucifer. He had already alienated a company of the angels under his leadership before he turned his attention to the human race.

Genesis 3:1–13 records how Lucifer, appearing in the form of a serpent, approached Adam and Eve, the parents of the human race, and enticed them into rebellion. In response, God pronounced a prophetic judgment on Lucifer and on the woman:

> So the LORD God said to the serpent: "Because you have done this, you are cursed more than all cattle, and more than every beast of the field; on your belly you shall go, and you shall eat dust all the days of your life. And I will put enmity between you and the woman, and between

your seed and her Seed; He shall bruise your head, and
you shall bruise His heel."

verses 14–15

This is the first instance in Scripture of direct predictive
prophecy concerning future events. It focused on two persons: the descendant of the serpent and the descendant of
the woman. It predicted what would become an ongoing
conflict between them, with the result that the heel of the
woman's descendant would be bruised but the head of
the serpent would be crushed. While the bruising of the
heel would not be a final defeat, the crushing of the head
would be. A serpent with a crushed head has been put
out of action.

Adam and Eve had fallen into Satan's trap. It would seem
that God's predetermined purpose had been frustrated.
Similar situations occur in later prophetic revelations. But
it is characteristic of God in such cases that He has a "secret plan." In fact, God always anticipates the crisis and
has His own response prepared in His mind—often a long
time beforehand. In this case, the woman's descendant was
revealed in history as Yeshua Ben David—Jesus, Son of
David. The prophecy concerning the bruising of the heel
of the woman's descendant was fulfilled in the suffering
that Jesus endured for our redemption. Its final outworking made salvation available to every descendant of Adam
who would fulfill the required conditions.

It is a common mistake for people approaching the Bible
to assume that it is a condensed history of the universe,
but this is not so. It is the history of a certain man named
Adam and his descendants. Other aspects of history are

included only because they help us to understand God's dealings with Adam.

Failure to understand this special purpose for which the Bible was written has been a source of many—but not all—apparent conflicts between the record of Scripture and secular science. The focus of science is general. It includes the entire history of the universe. The focus of Scripture, on the other hand, is limited and specific. It deals with one man, Adam, and his descendants. It has nothing to say about any other races that may have existed. It does not deny their existence, but it has little or nothing to say about them.

Why should this one man, Adam, be so important? Because God, in His eternal counsel, had determined that through Adam's descendants He would send to earth His unique and only begotten Son—the Lord Jesus. This makes the destiny of the Adamic race different from that of all other races that have ever existed.

Remember that "Adam" is a proper name. Wherever we read in the Old Testament the "sons of men," it actually says the "sons of Adam." The central theme of the Bible is this one man Adam and his descendants. I believe that the method of Adam's creation and his relationship with God that developed out of it were unique.

However, I know of nothing in Scripture that implies that Adam was the first or the only being of a type similar to human who ever lived on the earth. I think it is entirely possible that there were one or more other races before Adam, but the Bible does not deal with them. The Bible is primarily a revelation given to us as members of the Adamic race to tell us things that we need to know for our spiritual benefit.

Other important facts are contained in this revelation, but they are really like the frame around a picture. The picture itself is Adam and his descendants and God's dealings with them. The other things that are revealed are not so much part of the picture as of the frame. To see the picture clearly, we have to get the frame right. But bear this in mind: The Bible is speaking primarily of Adam and his descendants.

One of the main titles given to Jesus in the New Testament is "the Son of Man." This title is a direct translation from the Hebrew phrase *Ben Adam*—that is, "Son of Adam." Actually, Jesus Himself used this title more than eighty times in the gospels. He deliberately declared Himself to be the Son of Adam.

> The Bible is primarily a revelation given to us as members of the Adamic race to tell us things that we need to know for our spiritual benefit.

Later on, in 1 Corinthians 15:45, the apostle Paul calls Jesus the "last Adam." In biological descent, Jesus was by no means the final representative of the Adamic race. Many thousands of descendants of Adam have been born since His time. But He was the "last" in the sense that He fully and finally exhausted the evil that had been brought upon His race.

Confronted with the rebellion of both Adam and Eve, God set in motion His "secret plan" conceived in eternity. Historically this plan was unfolded in the life, death and resurrection of Jesus. Jesus, the Son of Adam, was God's "secret weapon."

I know of no way to give an exact chronological date for the six days that culminated in the creation of Adam.

In the seventeenth century, Archbishop Ussher of the Anglican Church published a work entitled "Annals of the Old and New Testament." Working from the King James Version, he calculated that the date of the creation described in Genesis was 4004 BC. In the first Bible that I owned—given me by my grandmother—this date is actually printed in the margin.

Many Christians, however, no longer take this date seriously. The Bible leaves open the possibility that the creation described in Genesis 1:2 and following was preceded by an undetermined period of history. It could be thousands of years, or it could be millions of years. In my opinion, years are not relevant to measuring that period.

Scholars have come forward with various different interpretations of the opening verses of the Bible. Secular science, too, has made its contribution, which cannot be ignored. For my part, I know of nothing that precludes the possibility of successive periods of divine activity prior to the creation of Adam. I would refer to this as "a pre-Adamic period." Before we (Adam and his descendants) came on the scene there are indications that something had been going on for a very long time. If we could see that period as God sees it, we might classify it, subdivide it and recognize various different periods or ages.

I want to focus only on one aspect of the scriptural account: the creation of the heavens and then the earth.

In the opening verse of Scripture, we encounter one of those tremendous statements that never lose their impact. If there were only one verse in the Bible, and it was Genesis

1:1, I personally would acknowledge that it was inspired. To me it speaks with authority. Even as an unbeliever and a skeptic, I never could get away from the fact that there was authority here that I would have to face up to. And in due course, I did!

Here is the statement that confronts us: *In the beginning God created the heavens and the earth*. Let us focus for a moment on the order of events indicated here.

> If there were only one verse in the Bible, and it was Genesis 1:1, I personally would acknowledge that it was inspired.

When the Angels Sang

Various passages of Scripture indicate that God first created the heavens and the beings that were to inhabit the heavens. Then He created the earth. The heavens and their inhabitants were already in place when the earth was created.

In various places in the book of Job, we find Job arguing with the Lord. He was complaining that God was not running the universe according to Job's satisfaction. Things were getting out of hand and God was not treating Job as he felt he ought to be treated. Job was wishing that he could have a personal interview with the Lord.

Then in the midst of all this, the Lord suddenly came on the scene—in person—giving Job the shock of his life. The Lord started firing a series of questions at Job that he could not answer:

"Where were you when I laid the foundations of the earth?
Tell Me, if you have understanding. Who determined its
measurements? . . . Or who stretched the line [the architect's line] upon it? To what were its foundations fastened?
Or who laid its cornerstone, when the morning stars sang
together, and all the sons of God shouted for joy?"

Job 38:4–7

We see that when the Lord laid the foundations of the
earth, "the morning stars sang" and "the sons of God
shouted for joy"! Undoubtedly, in this context, the "sons
of God" are the angels. When God laid the foundations
of the earth, the angels were all watching. Heaven and its
hosts were already complete, and they all enjoyed the wonderful spectacle of the Lord bringing the earth into being.

Later, in dedicating his Temple, Solomon said to the
Lord: "But will God indeed dwell with men on the earth? Behold, heaven and the heaven of heavens cannot contain You.
How much less this temple which I have built!" (2 Chronicles 6:18). When Solomon speaks about the "heaven of
heavens," he depicts a heaven that is high above the heaven
that we see.

In a parallel passage in Nehemiah 9:6, Nehemiah takes
up this theme:

"You alone are the LORD; You have made heaven, the heaven
of heavens, with all their host, the earth and everything on
it, the seas and all that are in them, and You preserve them
all. The host of heaven worships You."

Nehemiah, like Solomon, speaks about "heaven" and
also the "heaven of heavens." This confirms that there is

a heaven that is as far above the one we see as the heaven that we see is above earth!

Mysteries Unfolded in Grammar

In the opening chapters of Genesis, certain significant words are plural in form, but are not easily identified when translated into English or another language. In the English language to make a noun plural, we normally add *s*. For example, the word *book* becomes *books, job* becomes *jobs* and so on. In the Hebrew language, one primary way to form the plural is by adding two letters, *im,* which are pronounced *eem*. This ending, *im,* is a normal plural form in Hebrew. In this very first verse of Scripture, we have two words ending in *im*. The word for *God* (*Elohim*) and the word for *heavens* (*shamaim*) are both plural in form.

Furthermore, Hebrew verbs also have a singular and plural form, which should agree with the nouns or pronouns to which they apply. Yet here in Genesis 1:1 we have an immediate conflict of grammar, because the Hebrew verb *created* is singular in form while the word for *God,* as already indicated, is plural! Here then is the mystery of the Triune God unfolded in the opening verse of Scripture: *In God there is both plurality and unity.*

As mentioned, *heaven* is also plural—*heavens* (*shamaim*), not *heaven*. The Bible clearly indicates (as we have seen and will see in subsequent sections of this book) that there is more than one heaven. On the other hand, the word for *earth* is singular. Thus we find that two words, *God* and *heaven,* are plural in form.

Two other words that also occur in Genesis are plural in form. First is the word *life* (*chaim*): "And the LORD God formed man of the dust of the ground, and breathed into his nostrils the breath of *life*; and man became a living being" (Genesis 2:7, emphasis added).

God breathed into Adam the breath of "lives." We find, as we go on throughout Scripture, that there are various forms of life: spiritual life and physical life, mortal life and immortal life. All these concepts are contained in seed form in this chapter of Genesis and developed in the subsequent unfolding of Scripture.

Another significant Hebrew word that occurs early in Genesis and that is plural in form is the word for *water* (*maim*): "And the Spirit of God was hovering over the face of the waters" (Genesis 1:2).

The Bible indicates there is more than one kind of water. There is water of life and there is natural water. There is water above the heavens and water under the heavens. The final promise of God concerning water is given in Revelation 22:17: "Whoever desires, let him take the *water of life* freely [without charge]" (emphasis added).

In every case in Scripture where a word is in the plural form, there is a good reason for it. In fact, revelation is contained even in that grammatical fact—that a noun is plural in form.

God Did Not Create a Mess

Returning to the opening verses of Genesis, I am forced to the conclusion that there is a contrast between the condition of the earth as originally created by God in verse 1 and its condition as described in verse 2:

[1] In the beginning God created the heavens and the earth.

[2] The earth was without form, and void; and darkness was on the face of the deep.

The earth as described in verse 2 had become a dark, formless, watery waste. Everything I read in the Bible from that verse onward convinces me that this is not a description of the earth as originally created by God. He is not an "experimenter," He is a Creator. Every other creative act of God described in this section of Scripture produced something perfect. It did not need to be improved on or repaired.

It becomes apparent, therefore, that this description of the earth given in verse 2 does not depict the earth in the state in which God originally created it as described in verse 1. On the contrary, it is a description of the earth in a state into which it was plunged as a result of things that happened between verses 1 and 2. It could indicate that something cataclysmic happened, which changed the order and beauty of the earth that God originally brought forth, and, as a result, it became a formless void. The word translated in this verse "*was* without form" could equally well be translated "*became* without form."

> God is not an "experimenter," He is a Creator.

The language used in the Hebrew is striking. "Without form, and void" translates the Hebrew phrase *tohu va-bohu*. These two rhyming words are designed to go together: *tohu* and *bohu*. Various other languages contain words that are paired like this. In English, for example, we have the phrase *harum-scarum*. In Russian there is a phrase for *upside-down*: *shiverit naviverit*. The rhyming phrases in these English and Russian examples are similar to the Hebrew phrase *tohu va-bohu*. It describes a disorderly condition. In fact, the words themselves contain the sense or feeling of the situation they describe.

Now let us examine the other places in the Old Testament where these same Hebrew words are used—*tohu* and *bohu*. There are only two other passages where both words are used together. The first is in Isaiah 34. This chapter depicts a future judgment of God on the territory of Edom, which is the name given to Jacob's twin brother, Esau, and his descendants. Edom is the country east of the Dead Sea. The Scripture indicates that at the close of this age there will be a terrible, desolating, permanent judgment of God upon the area. Edom will be judged in such a way as to be a perpetual monument of God's judgment for all successive generations. The description is very vivid:

> For it is the day of the Lord's vengeance, the year of recompense for the cause of Zion. Its streams shall be turned into pitch, and its dust into brimstone; its land shall become burning pitch. It shall not be quenched night or day; its smoke shall ascend forever. From generation to generation it shall lie waste; no one shall pass through it forever and ever.
>
> Isaiah 34:8–10

It is the following verse that contains the phrase *tohu va-bohu*:

> But the pelican and the porcupine shall possess it, also the owl and the raven shall dwell in it. And He shall stretch out over it the line of confusion [*tohu*] and the stones of emptiness [*bohu*].
>
> verse 11

This is a metaphor from the architect's measuring line and plummet. With the measuring line he measures horizontally, and with the plummet he measures vertically. God's judgment is summed up in this descriptive phrase. It will be the measuring line of "confusion" (*tohu*) and the plummet of "emptiness" (*bohu*). In other words, what is it going to be? *Total desolation.* Edom will be completely given over to a desolation that will be a memorial of God's judgment forever afterward. The whole picture is one of God's anger and wrath released in a desolating judgment.

The other place where these two words—*tohu* and *bohu*—are found together is Jeremiah 4:22–23 where again the association of the words is with judgment. The judgment here described relates to Israel. In Jeremiah 4:22, God reveals the reason for His judgment: "For My people are foolish, they have not known Me. They are silly children, and they have no understanding. They are wise to do evil, but to do good they have no knowledge."

This is a picture of pervasive rebellion and wickedness. Then Jeremiah is given a vision of judgment to come: "I beheld the earth, and indeed it was without form [*tohu*], and void [*bohu*]; and the heavens, they had no light" (verse 23).

Here we see it again, "without form, and void"—*tohu* and *bohu*. It is a picture of desolation resulting from God's judgment upon wickedness.

In all Scripture there are only three places where these two words *tohu* and *bohu* occur together: Genesis 1:2, Isaiah 34:11, Jeremiah 4:23. The two latter Scriptures depict a fearful scene of desolation brought about by God's judgment upon terrible wickedness. We bring Genesis 1:2 exactly into line with these other two passages if we interpret it also to be a picture of God's judgment on acts of wickedness that in this verse are not described in detail.

Now let us examine some of the passages where *tohu* is used without *bohu*. Deuteronomy 32:10 says the Lord found Jacob "in a desert land and in the wasteland, a howling wilderness." The word *waste* is *tohu*. The whole picture is one of desolation.

In Job 6:18 we read of streams in the desert that dry up and run out onto the sand with nothing to offer anybody: "The paths of their way turn aside, they go nowhere and perish." The word *perish* is *tohu*. All that is left is sand.

In Job 12:24 and Psalm 107:4 the word *tohu* is translated "wilderness": "He takes away the understanding of the chiefs of the people of the earth, and makes them wander in a pathless wilderness [*tohu*]" (Job 12:24); "They wandered in the wilderness [*tohu*] in a desolate way" (Psalm 107:4).

In each of these cases, God's judgment produces a condition described as a wilderness (*tohu*).

If we combine all these passages quoted above, we arrive at one conclusion that applies to them all: They describe the result of a judgment of God. This could be applied as much to Genesis 1:2 as to the other passages.

We can also look at a number of instances in Isaiah that depict God's judgment on the whole earth: "Behold, the LORD makes the earth empty and makes it waste, distorts its surface and scatters abroad its inhabitants" (Isaiah 24:1).

As part of this total judgment, Isaiah goes on to say: "The city of confusion [*tohu*] is broken down" (verse 10). This depicts a city in a state of desolation as a result of God's judgment.

Again, Isaiah 40:23 depicts God's judgment on earth's rulers: "He brings the princes to nothing; He makes the judges of the earth useless [*tohu*]."

In Isaiah 41:29 God describes the worshipers of idols: "Indeed they are all worthless; their works are nothing; their molded images are wind and confusion [*tohu*]."

In every case, confusion is the outcome of God's wrath and judgment.

The most decisive statement of all is Isaiah 45:18:

> For thus says the LORD, who created the heavens, who is God, who formed the earth and made it, who has established it, who did not create it in vain [*tohu*], who formed it to be inhabited: "I am the LORD, and there is no other."

The product of God's creation was not *tohu*—that is, in a confused, disorderly condition.

Let us now put this passage of Scripture side by side with that which describes God's creation.

Genesis 1:2 says that the earth was *tohu*. Isaiah 45:18 says that God did not create it *tohu*. The implication is clear: The earth as described in Genesis 1:2 is not in the condition in which it was originally created. God did not create an earth that was *tohu* and *bohu,* but He created it to be inhabited. His aim was to make a blessed, pleasant, wonderful place for His creatures to dwell in.

The fact that the earth became *tohu* and *bohu* indicates that a judgment of God had passed over it between its creation as recorded in Genesis 1:1 and the scene depicted in Genesis 1:2. In our next chapter, we will analyze the biblical record of a rebellion of angels that provoked God's judgment. This could well have taken place in the period between Genesis 1:1 and Genesis 1:2.

> But we should never allow the things we do not understand to obscure for us the areas of truth where God has provided clear understanding.

Confronted with this picture of *tohu* and *bohu,* we might ask: Could this perhaps in some way be connected with what scientists have come to interpret as the "Big Bang"? This would view it not primarily as an act of creation, but as an act of judgment.

I certainly do not claim to have answered all the questions that arise about creation. In fact, there is no limit to such questions. But we should never allow the things we do not understand to obscure for us the areas of truth where God has provided clear understanding.

In closing this chapter, let me share with you something I have proved over the years. God does not necessarily commit Himself to scratch every intellect that itches, but He will always respond to a sincere and hungering heart.

We will now go on to examine the confrontation between God and Lucifer that brought judgment upon God's original creation.

Questions for This Study

1. Give the various words and meanings used for *tohu* and *bohu* given throughout this chapter.

   Tohu: _____

   Bohu: _____

2. Where did rebellion begin, and who led it?

   In _____ by _____.

3. What is the primary nature of the Bible?

   _____

   _____

4. We should never allow the things we _____ _____ _____ to obscure for us the _____ _____ _____ where God has provided _____ _____.

Life Application

1. How has reading about the pre-Adamic world helped your concept of creation?

2. What has it done to show the importance of "rightly dividing" the Word of God? (See 2 Timothy 2:15.)

Notes

_____

_____

_____

_____

Memory Verse

"Now then, my sons, listen to me [wisdom]; blessed are those who keep my ways. Listen to my instruction and be wise; do not ignore it. Blessed is the man who listens to me, watching daily at my doors, waiting at my doorway."

Proverbs 8:32–34 NIV

Faith Response

Father, there is so much in Your Word for me to discover. I thank You, Holy Spirit, for being here to teach me and bring me revelation and understanding. Guide me in this study to grasp everything You have for me.

4 Lucifer Challenges God

"I saw Satan fall like lightning from heaven."
Luke 10:18

Jesus is here describing for His disciples a scene He had witnessed in heaven many centuries before His incarnation as the Son of Mary. He was warning them of the danger of pride. The scene He described was God's judgment on a created archangel named Lucifer.

Lucifer had occupied a position of unique honor in heaven. God had said to him:

"You were the seal of perfection, full of wisdom and perfect in beauty. You were in Eden, the garden of God; every precious stone was your covering: the sardius, topaz, and diamond, beryl, onyx, and jasper, sapphire, turquoise, and emerald with gold. The workmanship of your timbrels and pipes was prepared for you on the day you were created. You were the anointed cherub who covers; I established you; you were on the holy mountain of God; you walked back and forth in the midst of fiery stones. You were perfect in your ways from the day you were created, till iniquity was found in you."

Ezekiel 28:12–15

This account raises two possible questions. First, from what area of heaven was Lucifer cast out? Second, to what area was he cast down?

Personally, I do not believe that Lucifer had access to the third heaven or could ever have conceived his rebellion there. My impression of the third heaven is that it is a place of such total holiness that no kind of sin could ever begin to exist there. But that is just a personal impression!

I have not found any passage in Scripture that describes the specific location to which Lucifer and his angels were banished, but apparently they set up their rival kingdom in another area of the heavenlies, probably somewhere in the mid-heaven.

As I pointed out in chapter 1, in Scripture at least three different areas are called "heaven." First the visible heaven above us. Next comes the mid-heaven described in Revelation 8:13; 14:6; and 19:17. Finally, the third heaven is the highest of all and is the sacred place of God's dwelling, the place that Solomon refers to in 2 Chronicles 2:6 as the "heaven of heavens": "But who is able to build Him a temple, since heaven and the heaven of heavens cannot contain Him?"

In Ezekiel 28:14, Lucifer is described as the "anointed cherub who covers." It seems that Lucifer had covered with his wings the place of the manifestation of God's glory in His heavenly temple, just as the cherubs in the tabernacle of Moses covered the mercy seat and the place where the visible glory of God appeared. This is described in Exodus 37:9: "The cherubim spread out their wings above, and covered the mercy seat with their wings. They faced one another; the faces of the cherubim were toward the mercy seat."

Lucifer was perfect in beauty, but he was a created being. Pride motivated him to challenge God and to claim a place of equality with God. Apparently Lucifer had authority over a company of angels, and he had succeeded in alienating some of those under him from their loyalty to God. He led them to join him in his rebellion against God. In response, God cast Lucifer and his partners in rebellion from His presence.

To describe Lucifer's activity in turning some angels against God, Scripture uses the word *trading*, which could also apply to *persistent plotting*:

"By the abundance of your *trading* you became filled with violence within, and you sinned. . . . You defiled your sanctuaries by the multitude of your iniquities, by the iniquity of your *trading*."

Ezekiel 28:16, 18, emphasis added

This word *trading* is also applied to someone who goes about as a *talebearer* or a *slanderer*. In other words, it could describe someone who peddles both goods and gossip. In various other books of the Bible—e.g., Leviticus, Proverbs, Jeremiah—this word is translated as either a "talebearer" or a "slanderer." For example, Leviticus 19:16 says: "You shall not go about as a talebearer among your people."

In Proverbs 20:19, this practice of being a talebearer is closely linked with one who flatters with his lips. We are warned against both kinds of persons: "He who goes about as a talebearer reveals secrets; therefore do not associate with one who flatters with his lips."

Apparently, this exactly describes what Lucifer did. He went among the created angelic beings, promoting and organizing rebellion against God. I personally picture Lucifer as saying to the angels under him such things as, "God does not really appreciate you. You have a position that is far below your potential and far below what you should have. If I were to take over, I would understand your merits and your value and I would promote you. I would give you a much more responsible position in the government of the universe."

Obviously all this did not happen suddenly, or even in a few days. We have no way to measure the time it took Lucifer to promote his rebellion, but it was long enough for him to organize a carefully planned revolt against God and to persuade an estimated one-third of the angels to join him.

This estimate is based on a statement concerning Satan in Revelation 12:4: "His tail drew *a third* of the stars of heaven and threw them to the earth" (emphasis added). It interprets the phrase *the stars of heaven* as referring to the whole company of angels. But this interpretation could be questioned.

Perhaps you have never envisaged behavior like this among angels in heaven. As I mentioned earlier, however, the rebellious acts that it produced originated in heaven and not on earth. Furthermore, the devil has never had to change his tactics either in heaven or on earth for one simple reason: *because they still work!* As a master of slander or talebearing, he continues to seek to undermine various forms of authority that God has established both in the Church and in the world.

> The devil has never had to change his tactics either in heaven or on earth for one simple reason: **because they still work!**

When Lucifer was cast out of heaven, he did not terminate his rebellion, but he continued it by setting up a kingdom of his own in opposition to God's Kingdom. In Luke 11:17–18, Jesus reveals that Satan has a kingdom of his own: "Every kingdom divided against itself is brought to desolation, and a house divided against a house falls. If Satan also is divided against himself, how will his kingdom stand?"

Kingdoms in the Heavenlies

In Colossians 1:16, Paul outlines the governmental structure of God's Kingdom in heaven as it was originally established through Jesus in His eternal nature: "For by Him [Jesus] all things were created that are in heaven and that are on earth, visible and invisible, whether thrones or dominions or principalities or powers."

Note these four descending levels of authority. In each case, where appropriate, an alternative English translation is supplied in parenthesis:

Thrones
Dominions (lordships)
Principalities (rulerships)
Powers (authorities)

One major feature of Lucifer's rebellion was to take over the original governmental structure of God that he was familiar with and to use it against God. In Ephesians 6:12, Paul lists the main governmental structure of Satan's rebellious kingdom:

> For we do not wrestle against flesh and blood, but against principalities, against powers, against the rulers of the darkness of this age, against spiritual hosts of wickedness in the heavenly places.

In this list Paul makes no mention of "thrones" or "dominions." The implication is that these two highest ranks did not associate themselves with Lucifer in his rebellion. Rebellion is depicted as beginning at the level of "principalities" (rulerships) and "powers" (authorities).

Pride: The Original Sin

Let us return to our passage in Ezekiel 28, which describes Lucifer's rebellion: "Your heart was lifted up [you became proud] because of your beauty; you corrupted your wisdom for the sake of your splendor" (verse 17).

Lucifer's heart was lifted up in pride because of his beauty and this was the reason that he was cast out of the mountain of God. I believe it is vitally important for all of us to realize that the first sin in the universe was not murder, nor adultery, but rather *pride*. It was pride that produced rebellion. Furthermore, it was pride arising from the blessings of which God Himself was the Author.

It was God who gave Lucifer his power, his authority, his beauty, his wisdom—all those were gifts from God. Yet Lucifer's wrong attitude turned them into instruments for his own destruction.

I look back now over more than sixty years in Christian service and I am shocked to realize that men and women called and equipped by God are still today making the same tragic error that Lucifer made. I am reminded continually of a Chinese pastor who spent more than twenty years in prison for his faith. He said, "I've seen many Christians have a good beginning, but few have a good ending." How quickly and easily, as God's servants, we tend to forget that every success in our ministry should prompt us to self-humbling in response to God's unmerited favor!

In Isaiah 14:12–15, the prophet analyzes the motive behind Lucifer's rebellion. It was an ambition to be equal with God:

> I believe it is vitally important for all of us to realize that the first sin in the universe was not murder, nor adultery, but rather **pride.**

"How you are fallen from heaven, O Lucifer, son of the morning! How you are cut down to the ground, you who weakened the nations! For you have said in your heart: 'I will ascend into heaven, I will exalt my throne above the stars of God; I will also sit on the mount of the congregation on the farthest sides of the north; I will ascend above the heights of the clouds, I will be like [or equal to] the Most High.' Yet you shall be brought down to Sheol, to the lowest depths of the Pit."

As quoted above, Lucifer made five successive declarations prefaced by the phrase *I will*. He said, "*I will* ascend into heaven . . . *I will* exalt my throne . . . *I will* sit on the mount of the congregation . . . *I will* ascend above the heights of the clouds." Finally comes the climax, "*I will* be like [or equal to] the Most High," like God Himself. Lucifer's self-promoting ambition was the cause of his fall.

Scripture confronts us with a deliberate contrast between Lucifer and Jesus. Lucifer was not in the form of God; he was a created being. He had no right to be equal with God. Yet he grasped at equality with God, and when he reached up, he slipped and fell. On the other hand, Jesus was divine by eternal nature and enjoyed equality with God. He did not need to grasp at it, but rather, He humbled Himself.

Jesus: The Pattern of Humility

Paul vividly depicts the self-humbling of Jesus in Philippians 2:

68

Who, being in the form of God, did not consider it robbery to be equal with God, but made Himself of no reputation, taking the form of a bondservant, and coming in the likeness of men. And being found in appearance as a man, He humbled Himself and became obedient to the point of death, even the death of the cross.

verses 6–8

An alternative translation for ". . . did not consider it robbery to be equal with God" would be ". . . did not count equality with God a thing to be seized."

These verses outline for us seven great downward steps that Jesus took from heaven's glory to His death on the cross:

- *He made Himself of no reputation.* Literally, He *emptied* Himself. As Charles Wesley says in one of his hymns, "[Christ] emptied Himself of all but love."
- *He took upon Himself the form of a servant.* He was the "LORD of glory," but He stepped down to become a servant.
- *He was made in the likeness of men.* He became a member of the Adamic race, made a little lower than the angels.
- *He was found in fashion (appearance) as a man.* He looked just like a normal man of His own day. There was nothing external to distinguish Him from the people He lived among.
- *He humbled Himself.* He was a humble man. He was not a priest or a ruler, but a carpenter's son.

- *He became obedient unto death.* His perfect obedience brought Him ultimately to His atoning death for sinful humanity.
- *He became obedient to the death of a criminal on the cross.* Crucifixion was the agonizing penalty for the worst person who had committed the most heinous crime.

Those are the seven great downward steps that the Lord Jesus took. But the seven great downward steps led to the seven great upward steps that are described in verses 9–11:

> Therefore God also has highly exalted Him and given Him the name which is above every name, that at the name of Jesus every knee should bow, of those in heaven, and of those on earth, and of those under the earth, and that every tongue should confess that Jesus Christ is Lord, to the glory of God the Father.

Here we have the seven upward steps of the exaltation of Jesus:

- *God has highly exalted Him.*
- *God has given Him a name that is above every name.*
- *At the name of Jesus, every knee shall bow.*
- *"Of those in heaven"*—that is, all the created hosts who serve God in His heaven.
- *"Of those on earth."* This means that ultimately every creature on earth will submit to the authority of Christ.
- *"Of those under the earth."* This refers to Satan's realm in Hades. It includes death, hell, the grave and

also the unrighteous dead who had previously rejected God's mercy.

• *Every tongue shall confess that Jesus Christ is Lord.* The Lordship of Jesus will be proclaimed in every area of the universe.

In all of this, the perfect pattern set before us is Jesus. Paul encourages us as followers of Jesus to humble ourselves:

Let nothing be done through selfish ambition or conceit, but in lowliness of mind let each esteem others better than himself. Let each of you look out not only for his own interests, but also for the interests of others. Let this mind be in you which was also in Christ Jesus.

Philippians 2:3–5

The two motivations that Paul rules out are self-centered ambition and conceit. There is only one pathway to promotion: self-humbling. In Luke 14:11, Jesus states this principle very clearly: "For whoever exalts himself will be humbled, and he who humbles himself will be exalted."

This is an absolutely unvarying principle. There are no exceptions! *The way up is down.* That is the great secret! As Proverbs 18:12 declares: "Before honor is humility."

> There is only one pathway to promotion: self-humbling.

Referring again to Philippians, we see a wonderful truth brought to light: "*Therefore* God also has highly exalted Him [Jesus]" (2:9, emphasis added).

71

The word *therefore* leads me to believe that Jesus was not promoted because He was the favorite Son, but because He fulfilled the conditions. He had to *earn* His exaltation.

> Self-humbling is an issue of the will, not of the emotions.

We could presume that automatically at the end of His suffering on the cross He would return to His position of equality with God. But as I understand it, He had to earn that right by the way He humbled Himself. He earned it not merely for Himself, but for all who follow Him.

In response you may feel prompted to pray, "Lord, I need humility. Please make me humble." Surprisingly, however, God's answer will be, "I cannot do that. Only you can humble yourself."

Self-humbling is an issue of the will, not of the emotions. It is a decision each of us has to make for himself: "Lord, I choose to humble myself before You. I renounce pride, arrogance and personal ambition before You and before my fellow believers."

To give a practical example of self-humbling, Jesus spoke about guests invited to a wedding feast:

> "When you are invited by anyone to a wedding feast, do not sit down in the best place, lest one more honorable than you be invited by him; and he who invited you and him come and say to you, 'Give place to this man,' and then you begin with shame to take the lowest place. But when you are invited, go and sit down in the lowest place, so that when he who invited you comes he may say to you, 'Friend, go up higher.' Then you will have glory in the

presence of those who sit at the table with you. *For whoever exalts himself will be humbled, and he who humbles himself will be exalted.*"

Luke 14:8–11, emphasis added

At this point, each of us is confronted by the need to make a personal decision. I cannot make the decision for you and you cannot make the decision for me. But let me tell you, my decision has already been made.

How about you?

Questions for This Study

1. What does Satan seek as a master of slander or tale-bearing?

   _____

   _____

   _____

2. What was Lucifer's sin that produced rebellion?

   _____

3. What contrasts between Lucifer and Jesus can we draw from Isaiah 14:12–15 and Philippians 2:6–8?

   _____

   _____

   _____

   _____

4. What is the pathway to promotion? _____-_____

Life Application

1. What can you learn from the fact that pride arose in Lucifer from having been blessed by God, and how can you guard against it?

2. What can you do to maintain an attitude of humility?

Notes

_____

_____

_____

_____

_____

_____

Memory Verse

Do nothing out of selfish ambition or vain conceit, but in humility consider others better than yourselves. Each of you should look not only to your own interests, but also to the interests of others.

Philippians 2:3–4 NIV

Faith Response

Father, I do humble myself here before You. I acknowledge that You are God, my provider of everything. Every good and perfect gift comes from You.

I was in need of a Savior and You sent Jesus. It is Your love, grace and mercy that keep me. You have lavished Your grace on me, and I don't deserve it. I am nothing without You, but in You, I have everything. Thank You, Father.

5   The Adamic Race: *Our Origin*

God had been confronted by rebellion amongst angelic beings—beings of amazing beauty and strength and intelligence.

How did God respond? Did He bring into being still more majestic heavenly hosts—creatures of even greater beauty and strength and intelligence? Certainly He could have done so had He desired. But, in fact, He did the very opposite. He reached down and not up.

He created a new race from the lowliest source available—from the earth. The name of the being He created was "Adam." This name is derived directly from the Hebrew word *adamah,* meaning "earth." The Adamic race is the *earthy* race. Yet the unfolding revelation of Scripture makes it clear that God had in mind for the Adamic race a destiny higher than that of the angels.

It is important to realize that the creation of Adam and the Adamic race was part of God's response to Satan's rebellion. In a certain sense, this new race was designed to fulfill the destiny from which Satan had fallen and even to go beyond that. This is one main reason why Satan opposes our race with such intense hatred. He sees us as those who will supplant him and enter into a destiny that he failed to achieve. What is that destiny?

To understand our *destiny,* which we will explore in the next chapter, we must first understand our *origin—how and why mankind was created.* Both our origin and our destiny are revealed in the opening chapters of the book of Genesis.

The opening verse of the book of Genesis states: "In the beginning God created the heavens and the earth" (Genesis 1:1). Further on in Genesis 1:26–27 it describes the creation of man: "Then God said, 'Let Us make man in Our image, according to Our likeness. . . . ' So God created man in His own image; in the image of God He created him; male and female He created them." We need to set the creation of man against a historical background extending over vast periods of time.

At the End of the Ages

God works according to a chronological system that He Himself has devised. It is important to find out where we are at this time in God's chronology. Concerning the coming of Jesus to earth, we are told in Hebrews 9:26: ". . . but now, once *at the end of the ages,* He has appeared to put away sin by the sacrifice of Himself" (emphasis added). This indicates that the coming of Jesus to earth is the culmination of a program that God has been following over a period described as "the ages." In 1 Corinthians 10:11 Paul says that all these things "were written for our admonition, upon whom *the ends of the ages* have come" (emphasis added). The Church of the New Testament obviously understood that it was destined to be the climax of divine purposes that had been initiated in earlier ages.

These Scriptures indicate that the coming of Jesus and the establishing of the Church are some of the final events that close a period described as "the ages." How are we to interpret that phrase *the ages*? In Psalm 90:4 the psalmist is speaking to God and he says: "For a thousand years in Your sight are *like* yesterday when it is past, and *like* a watch in the night" (emphasis added). In the culture of the Bible a period of twelve hours was divided into three "watches" of four hours each. In other words, a thousand years correspond to four hours. A 24-hour day would correspond to six thousand years.

We see, then, that the events described in Genesis 1:2 and following are the culmination of divine activity that goes back over a period of time much longer than our limited minds have any capacity to comprehend.

With this in mind, we will now turn to the opening verses of the book of Genesis. As we have seen, the first verse describes the original act of creation, and the first part of the second verse describes a subsequent condition of the earth: "The earth was without form, and void; and darkness was on the face of the deep."

In chapter 3 of this book, I have explained why I believe this "void" was not the condition of the earth as originally created, but rather the result of a tremendous judgment of

God that was brought upon the pre-Adamic earth, probably as a result of Satan's rebellion. This was a judgment on the wickedness of the pre-Adamic race (or races) then upon the earth who had been led by Satan in rebellion and into various forms of wickedness.

It would appear that the main instrument of judgment in this instance was water. The earth became a desolate, formless, watery waste, and darkness was upon the face of the waters. Then the second part of verse 2 says: "And the Spirit of God was hovering [brooding, almost like a bird] over the face of the waters."

> "Therefore, if anyone is in Christ, he is a **new creation**; old things have passed away; behold, all things have become new."

The emphasis is on darkness and water. From Genesis 1:3 ("Let there be light") onward as far as Genesis 2:7 ("And the LORD God formed man"), the theme is not primarily original creation, but essentially restoration. In most instances, the material was already there. It simply had to be re-formed and reshaped. I am not suggesting that no creative acts took place, but original creation was not a main feature.

Aside from the re-creation process that filled the earth with sea creatures and other living things, we must not miss the application of this creative process for us as Christians. In 2 Corinthians 5:17, Paul says: "Therefore, if anyone is in Christ, he is a *new creation*; old things have passed away; behold, all things have become new" (emphasis added).

In a certain sense, this new creation in Christ is a work of *restoration*. When I come to Christ as a sinner, my whole personality is not obliterated. God does not bring something totally new into being, but He sets in operation forces that will restore me, renew me and ultimately bring forth out of me something completely new. Therefore, the work of restoration described in Genesis 1 and 2 is extremely relevant and applicable to the new creation in Christ. That is one reason that Scripture records it in some detail.

Several aspects of the creation in Genesis 1:2 are reproduced in the restoration of a sinner when he comes to Christ. The "world" (or the "earth" as described in Genesis 1:2) was in a mess. Likewise, when you or I come to Jesus Christ as sinners, we may or may not know it, but we too are in a mess. Not only are we in a mess, but like the earth in Genesis 1:2, we are in the dark. While we are in the dark, we cannot see things as they really are. This was the condition of the earth and it is also the condition of the individual sinner.

> While we are in the dark, we cannot see things as they really are. This was the condition of the earth and it is also the condition of the individual sinner.

There are two great agents of restoration in the new creation. In Genesis 1:2, the *Spirit* of God was "hovering." In Genesis 1:3, God spoke and His *Word* went forth. It is by the union of the Word and the Spirit of God that creation and re-creation take place. What happens when a sinner comes to repentance? The Spirit of God begins to move on that sinner's heart and he receives the proclaimed Word of God. By the Spirit and the Word the process of re-creation (or restoration) in Christ is set in motion.

The first product of the union of the Spirit and the Word working together was *light*. Thereafter, God worked in the light. The first thing that happens when a sinner comes to Christ is that he begins to see things—and himself—the way they really are. From that point on God continues to work in his life in the light.

There follows a process of separation and refinement, distinction and multiplication. Many different areas are dealt with in a successive order. Sometimes we reach a stage where we think, *Now I'm really finished. God has dealt with everything.* It is right at this point that a new area in our lives is exposed and brought to light by the Spirit of God, and then He proceeds graciously to deal with that area.

This is how God worked in the restoration described in Genesis 1. He worked in stages: first the water, then the earth, then the vegetation, the fishes, the birds, then the beasts and so on. Finally, we come to the climax of the creative process: the creation of man.

First, let me say that the creation of man gives us this further astonishing revelation about God: There is *plurality* in God: "Then God said, 'Let *Us* make man in *Our* image, according to *Our* likeness'" (Genesis 1:26, emphasis added).

I have already pointed out that the word for *God* (*Elohim*) is plural in form. This agrees with the language that

God uses here about Himself, "Let *Us* make man in *Our* image." Some people say that this is just the regal form where the king speaks of himself in the plural, but this is ruled out by the fact that later on, when speaking about man's Fall, God says: "Then the LORD God said, 'Behold, the man has become like *one of Us,* to know good and evil'" (Genesis 3:22, emphasis added).

God is plural, but He is also *one*. The Hebrew word for *one* used here and applied to God is *echad*. It denotes a unity with component elements. In Genesis 2:24, the same word, *echad,* is used again: "Therefore a man shall leave his father and mother and be joined to his wife, and they [two] shall become one [*echad*] flesh."

The word used here, *echad,* is not the word for absolute indivisible unity, which is *yachid*. The Hebrew word used in this verse, *echad,* is applied to marriage. It describes a oneness that is made up of two distinct persons united. In the biblical revelation of God, however, there are not two, but three Persons united to produce oneness. Not an absolute oneness, but a oneness in which there is also plurality.

Some people object to the concept of a Triune God, but I see it clearly revealed in Scripture. I believe in God the Father, I believe in God the Son and I believe in God the Holy Spirit. What is more important, not merely do I believe in them, but I know each of them through direct, personal experience. I know what it is to have a relationship with the Father, I know what it is to have a relationship with the Son, and I know what it is to have a relationship with the Holy Spirit.

The Climax: In His Own Image

Genesis 1:27 describes the climax of the process by which God created man. "So God created man *in His own image*" (emphasis added). God did not rest in this creation process until He had brought forth His own likeness. In the new creation in Christ, likewise, God will not rest until He has brought forth in us His own likeness. This is His ultimate goal.

In Genesis 2:7, a new title is given to God: "The LORD God." The Hebrew actually says "Yahweh God" or "Jehovah God." As I mentioned earlier, most modern scholars prefer to use "Yahweh" rather than "Jehovah."

But whichever form is used, the most important fact is that it is a proper (personal) name.

In Genesis 1, we have only the name "God." But in Genesis 2 we have the sacred name "Yahweh" added. This is significant because Genesis 1 describes general creation, whereas in Genesis 2 the emphasis is on the creation of Adam as a person. The introduction of the personal name of God, "Yahweh," emphasizes that God, as a Person, created Adam, as a person. This established a unique personal relationship between God, the Creator, and Adam, the creature.

There are further unique features of Adam that apparently distinguish him from any other creature of God. The most significant is the method of Adam's creation. "The LORD God ["Yahweh"] *formed* man of the dust of the ground" (Genesis 2:7, emphasis added).

The word *form* is normally used of a potter molding a clay vessel. The account depicts a vessel of clay being skillfully molded into the most perfect piece of statuary that earth had ever seen. Yet it was merely a lifeless form of clay until God imparted Himself to it: ". . . ["Yahweh God"] *breathed* into his nostrils the breath of life; and man became a living being [soul]" (Genesis 2:7, emphasis added).

In the original Hebrew, Genesis 2:7 is tremendously vivid and dramatic. In the Hebrew language, the sound of a word often depicts what the word describes. For instance, the Hebrew word for a *bottle* is *bak-buk,* which reproduces the gurgle of water being poured out of a bottle.

Similarly, where the Scripture says, "He breathed into his nostrils," the Hebrew word for *breathed* is *yi-pach.* Phonetically, the *p* sound in the middle is called a "plosive." In other words, it is produced by a miniature explosion—a sharp outgoing breath.

On the other hand, the Hebrew guttural sound *chet,* the *ch* at the end of *yi-pach,* consists of a continuing outgoing breath expelled from the throat. The total phrase *yi-pach* indicates there was a sharp expulsion of breath followed by a continuing outflow of air. It was not a gentle sigh. It was a sharp, authoritative expulsion of divine breath into the nostrils and mouth of that clay. It produced a living person—a human being—a living soul.

Think of the miracle this depicts—even in the physical realm! Think of the amazing fact that the little balls of clay turned into eyes, and that all the interior organs came into being, the heart began to beat, the blood began to circulate. Let me point out that if ever there was a logical basis for seeking healing from God, this is it! When your shoes need repair, you do not take them to the watchmaker.

No, you take them to the shoemaker. When your body is in need of restoration, the logical place to take it is to the One who created it, the body Maker. That is a solid basis for the ministry of healing through prayer.

> I have discovered in personal experience that God is still in the creating business.

I have discovered in personal experience that God is still in the creating business. I have frequently seen God do visible, creative miracles. One very unusual miracle I observed was God producing a nail on an index finger of a man where there never had been a nail. It happened in less than a second—to a Catholic priest! I have also seen scores of stunted legs grow out in front of my eyes. These were examples of the creative power of God in action. He has never retired from the creating business.

In John 9:1–7, when Jesus met a man born blind, He healed him in a remarkable way. He spat on the ground, made clay of the spittle and anointed the eyes of the blind man with the clay. He then sent him on his way saying, "Go, wash in the pool of Siloam."

Jesus could have healed that man in any number of ways, but He chose to do it that way. Why? Well, the man was born blind. His eyes had never had sight. I imagine maybe they were shriveled and wasted away. It was not just healing of a disease; it was really a creative act. Jesus served notice on His generation: "I am still the same One who made the clay in the Garden and breathed into it. When I mold clay and I breathe into it, creation takes place."

When God stooped down in the Garden and put His nostrils against those nostrils of clay, His lips against the lips of clay, and expelled His breath, man became a living soul.

The Breath of Lives

The opening chapters of Genesis reveal "life" on two different levels: the spirit and the soul. Each is vividly illustrated by the Hebrew word used. The Hebrew word for *spirit* is *ruach* in which the terminal letter, *chet,* depicts a continuing outflow dependent on no external source. On the other hand, the Hebrew word for *soul* is *nefesh*. This depicts life, which must receive before it can give. *Nefesh* begins with an intake of breath followed by a release of the breath that has been received.

In chapter 3, I pointed out that the opening chapters of Genesis contain certain words that are plural in form. This applies to the word *life* (*chaim*). There are two forms of life as we know it: the life of the spirit and the life of the soul. God breathed into Adam's nostrils the breath of lives (*chaim*)—life in all its forms.

The method of man's creation was unique. I am not talking now about the forming of his body from clay, but about the fact that God breathed life directly into him. In this way, God and man came into direct confrontation, face to face.

I believe this demonstrates that man, out of all creatures in the universe, has a unique capacity for direct access to the presence of God and for ongoing fellowship with God. This means that there is something in man that uniquely corresponds to something in God. It finds expression in one word: *fellowship*. The supreme purpose of the Gospel is to bring man back into fellowship with God.

This brings out a unique correspondence between the opening and the closing chapters of the Bible. The climax of the relationship that began in Genesis chapters 1 and 2 is depicted in Revelation 22:3–4, which is the last description in Scripture of God's redeemed people: "His servants shall serve Him. They shall see His face, and His name shall be on their foreheads."

Man at this point has been brought back into that direct, face-to-face fellowship with Almighty God for which he was created. The purposes of God that were temporarily frustrated by Satan are in the end perfectly fulfilled through Jesus Christ and His redemptive work. This makes man's relationship with God unique and decisive. He has a capacity for fellowship with God unequaled even by the angels. In eternity, the redeemed in Christ are going to be closer to God than the angels.

> One of the most amazing things to me in Scripture is how much God concerns Himself with man.

One of the most amazing things to me in Scripture is how much God concerns Himself with man. I cannot help but say with the psalmist: "What is man that You are mindful of him, and the son of man that You visit him?" (Psalm 8:4).

In other words, "Why do You spend so much trouble on us human beings?" Yet, as I understand Scripture objectively, we are the center of God's attention. We are the "apple" of His eye. In 1 Corinthians 3:21, Paul says to the Christians: "For *all* things are yours" (KJV, emphasis added). Everything, in heaven and on earth, belongs to us. Everything is at our disposal.

Personally, nothing grieves me more than to encounter Christians talking and acting as if they are unimportant. Such talk may sound humble, but it is actually unbelief. We *are* the most important people in the universe. Not because of what we are in ourselves, but because of Christ's redemptive work on our behalf. In Him we are created for a special relationship with God.

God's Image and God's Likeness

Genesis 1:26 reveals that there are two different aspects of the similarity between God and man. First, he was made in God's *image* (*tselem*) and second, he was made in God's *likeness* (*dmut*).

The word *image* (*tselem*) describes external form. It is the normal Hebrew word for *shadow,* and it is translated "shade" or "shadow" many times in the Old Testament. Interestingly enough, in a verbal form it recurs in the modern Hebrew word for "to have your photograph taken." Through more than 3,500 years, the Hebrew language has always used this word to refer to outward visible form.

Man represents God both inwardly and outwardly. In outward appearance, he looks like God. Some people have an idea of God as a kind of vague blurred mist. They cannot envisage Him with any definite external form. But the Bible reveals that God has a right hand, a left hand, He has ears and eyes, He has feet, He sits, He walks, He stands,

He has a back, He has a front. In all these respects, He is just like you and me. The contrary, however, is the real truth: It is not that God is like you and me, it is that you and I are like God.

In the human race, it is the male rather than the female that accurately represents God's external appearance. In 1 Corinthians 11:7, Paul explains it like this: "For a man indeed ought not to cover his head, since he is *the image and glory of God*; but woman is the glory of man" (emphasis added). It is important to emphasize that Paul is here speaking about the external, physical appearance, not about the inward, spiritual nature.

All this comes to a head in the account of the incarnation. God was incarnate in the Person of Jesus Christ. God took up His dwelling in man and was manifested in a body of flesh. It was appropriate that the body should be the body of a male human being.

In other words, there is something about the male human being that is specifically designed to manifest God. Even the angels do not have this unique function to show forth the visible likeness of God. That privilege is reserved for man. This is another reason why the devil hates men and will do everything he can to defile the image of God in man.

I once knew a young lady who was engaged to a young man and carried his photograph in her purse. One day she got a letter from her fiancé saying he had found someone else whom he intended to marry. When she got the news she took out his photograph and tore it into pieces and stamped on it. She could not touch him, but she could touch his image.

That is just how the devil reacts. Normally he cannot touch God, so what does he do? He takes the image of God—man—and tears it up and stamps on it. Every time a drunken man lurches down the street, staggering in the gutter and vomiting, that is the devil stamping on the image of God. In a certain sense, he says, "There You are, God. See what Your image is looking like now? That is what I feel about You. I cannot touch You, but I can certainly defile Your image."

There was a brief period when Satan could touch God. That was when Jesus came in human form and submitted Himself to Pilate's judgment. Then Satan was able to do what he really wanted to do—to God—in the Person of Jesus. The result was the crucifixion. But at all other times Satan is limited to doing the worst he can to human beings made to show forth the image of God.

Now let us examine *dmut,* the other Hebrew word used in Genesis 1:26 to describe man's resemblance to God. *Dmut* is a more general term than *tselem.* It does not refer primarily to outward appearance, but to man's whole person.

I have already pointed out that there is a tri-unity in God. There is a corresponding tri-unity in man. The three elements of his being are spirit, soul and body. In 1 Thessalonians 5:23, Paul prays for the Thessalonian Christians: "Now may the God of peace Himself sanctify you completely; and may your whole spirit, soul, and body be preserved blameless at the coming of our Lord Jesus Christ." Complete sanctification comprises all three elements: spirit, soul and body.

The spirit was breathed into man at creation by the Creator. His body was formed of clay from the ground.

The union of Spirit from above and clay from beneath produced a *soul*.

The soul is the individual ego in each one of us. The soul can say "I will" or "I will not." It is the decision-making element in our personalities. The soul operates the "rudder" by which we steer our way through life. In James 3:1–5, it is revealed that the "rudder" is the tongue.

> Salvation comes to the soul that makes the right decision in response to the Gospel and follows it through with an appropriate lifestyle.

Salvation comes to the soul that makes the right decision in response to the Gospel and follows it through with an appropriate lifestyle.

The union of God the Creator with a body of flesh produces the "new man." This new man is a moral being. Unlike an animal, he knows the difference between right and wrong, between good and evil. You can train a dog to do certain things and not to do other things. If the dog does one of the things he has been trained not to do and you discover it, he will put his tail between his legs and look guilty. But that is not evidence of a conscience that discerns between right and wrong. That is merely conditioning that determines behavior in certain situations. But man is created with a conscience that tells him that certain things are right and certain things are wrong.

Some people today are embracing a "new morality," which is actually as old as the Garden of Eden. In every generation, Satan seeks to blur the distinction between right and wrong, between good and evil. The fact remains that man does have a moral sense. He cannot get away from it. He can drink himself drunk; he can stupefy himself with drugs. But whatever he does, he cannot escape the fact that he knows there is right and he knows there is wrong.

Another distinctive feature of man is that he has a limited ability to create, which he has received from God. This is demonstrated in many ways. Man can plan and assemble and execute. For instance, if he wants to cross the sea, he can design and then construct a ship. He can see what items are needed; he can see how to assemble and fit them together. He can conceive and carry out a purpose.

In other words, man has a certain creative ability, which the lower animals do not have. A rabbit can build a burrow, a bird can build a nest, but they never change. They never develop. There is no progression. The ability to change and develop is confined to man.

In all three areas of his personality—spiritual, moral and intellectual—elements in man correspond uniquely to elements in God.

Questions for This Study

1. When you become a new creation in Christ, God sets forces in operation to help you in what ways?

_____

_____

2. What happens when sinners come to Christ?

_____

_____

_____

3. What finds expression in the word *fellowship* between God and man?

_____

4. To the soul that makes the _____ _____ in response to the _____ and follows through with an _____ _____, _____ comes.

Life Application

1. Compare your salvation experience and growth to the Genesis 1 account of creation and restoration described in this chapter.

2. Why are we the most important people in the universe?

Notes

_____

_____

_____

_____

_____

Memory Verse

When I consider your heavens, the work of your fingers, the moon and the stars, which you have set in place, what is man that you are mindful of him, the son of man that you care for him?

Psalm 8:3–4 NIV

Faith Response

Father, You are marvelous. You created everything in the universe, yet You love and care for mankind—for me. How amazing that I am the apple of Your eye! You watch over me, leading me and providing for me. Thank You, my wonderful Lord. I am humbled by the love You have for me and for all You have done.

6 The Adamic Race: *Our Destiny*

Looking beyond our origin, what is our destiny? We begin with the *purpose* for which man was created.

Simply put, man was created to be a ruler, to "have dominion." The second part of Genesis 1:26 says: "Let them have dominion over the fish of the sea, over the birds of the air, and over the cattle, over all the earth and over every creeping thing that creeps on the earth."

Notice that these words were not spoken of Adam as an individual, but of the race descended from him: "Let *them* have dominion. . . ."

The Adamic race was created to rule the entire globe—the sea, the earth, the air and all the creatures that inhabit these areas. Adam was to be God's visible representative exercising God-given authority over all the earth. When the other creatures on earth encountered Adam, they would recognize in him the likeness of the Creator as he exercised over them the dominion that the Creator had imparted to him.

This is brought out clearly in Psalm 8:4–8 (emphasis added):

> What is man that You are mindful of him, and the son of man that You visit him? For You have made him a little lower than the angels, and You have crowned him with glory and honor.
>
> You have made him to have *dominion* over the works of Your hands; You have put all things under his feet, all sheep and oxen—even the beasts of the field, the birds of the air, and the fish of the sea that pass through the paths of the seas.

These words are quoted in Hebrews 2:6–8 and applied to Jesus, but they are applied to Him as the head of the Adamic race. All has been put under the dominion of the Adamic race. In Jesus, the Adamic race found the fulfillment of its purpose. Prior to that, the purpose was stated but was not fulfilled. There is something even in fallen man that still knows he was created to rule. But his capacity to rule is impaired because of the work of sin in him.

> In Jesus, the Adamic race found the fulfillment of its purpose.

It is not surprising that man has explored the entire globe and even gone to the moon. It is an expression of the nature within him. He was made to explore, made to dominate, made to control. But he lacks divine authorization until he himself is under the control of God.

The next unique feature of Adam is what I call *intelligent partnership with God*. In this capacity, Adam was made responsible for the classification of the entire animal kingdom. This is recorded in Genesis 2:19–20:

> Out of the ground the LORD God formed every beast of the field and every bird of the air, and brought them to Adam to see what he would call them. And whatever Adam called each living creature, that was its name. So Adam gave names to all cattle, to the birds of the air, and to every beast of the field.

In the Hebrew language in which we receive the Bible, the giving of names is not done at random. It is never an accident. A name is always an expression of a nature. God brought the entire animal creation before Adam and commissioned him to "name" them. Adam gave them names, and whatever Adam called each one, that was its name.

Adam was able to give each animal its correct name. This indicated that Adam understood the relationships among the creatures: their orders, their species and so on. In other words, he had what we would call scientific knowledge, not by experiment, but by the exercise of divine revelation that stemmed from his relationship with God.

At Cambridge University I formerly held a studentship in philosophy, and I specialized in the study of the philosopher Plato. One of the things that Plato was most concerned with was the process of definition. I wrote my dissertation on "The Evolution of Plato's Method of Definition" and for this I was elected into a Fellowship in King's College, Cambridge. Plato discovered that we cannot satisfactorily define things by moving up from below, that is, from greater to lesser multiplicity. We cannot take a mass of different things and pick out all the similar features in them and eventually arrive at an exclusive list of things *common and peculiar* to that which we are seeking to define. No satisfactory definition can ever be achieved in that way. It is never adequate.

Ultimately Plato arrived at a conclusion, which makes him really the "father" of the method of definition by genus and species as it is used in modern science. Simply stated, we cannot begin from the bottom and work upward. We must begin from the top and work downward. We begin by establishing the family, then the genus, then the species and so on.

But how do we get the first stage—the all-inclusive classification? Plato's answer would be: by *intuition,* not by observation. This is an area where man has got to go above mere sense perception. Adam in his initial relationship with God had perfect intuition. He could see intuitively every relationship in the animal kingdom and then express it in the names that he gave.

The final unique feature of Adam in our study was *the provision of a mate.* Reading on in Genesis 2:20–24: "But for Adam there was not found a helper comparable to him" (verse 20).

The phrase *a helper comparable to him* in the Hebrew is *ezer k'negdo,* which more or less means "a helper to stand in front of him." When Adam had viewed all the animals, there was none to which he could relate in that personal way. To take him further, God had to put him to sleep.

And the LORD God caused a deep sleep to fall on Adam, and he slept; and He took one of his ribs, and closed up the flesh in its place. Then the rib which the LORD God had taken from man He made into a woman, and He brought her to the man.

And Adam said: "This is now bone of my bones and flesh of my flesh; she shall be called Woman [which in Hebrew is *ishah*], because she was taken out of Man [which in Hebrew is *ish*. There is a play on words]." Therefore a man shall leave his father and mother and be joined to his wife, and they shall become one flesh.

verses 21–24

Adam had been privileged to enjoy a unique presentation of the multifaceted order and perfection of God's creation. And yet there was still something missing. There was not any creature with which Adam could relate on his own level and share deeply all he was experiencing.

One of the most tantalizing things about scenes of extreme beauty is that it is difficult to enjoy them alone. There is something about real grandeur that you just cannot fully appreciate on your own. As a student at Cambridge, I had a friend who used to go walking with me in the mountains of Greece. But sometimes he would go off on his own. He particularly enjoyed the mountains of northwest Greece. He would just walk out with nothing but a sleeping bag. When night came, he would get inside his sleeping bag and lie there until the sun touched the mountains at dawn next day. Then he would come back and tell me, "It was so grand, it was so beautiful, but I just could not absorb it without somebody to share it with me."

I believe many of us are familiar with that kind of feeling. There comes a point when you say, "I must have someone to share it with."

After all the pageantry of the animal creation had passed before Adam, there still was not anybody with whom he could share it. God deliberately arranged it that way! He was showing Adam what He Himself wanted and He showed it by making Adam want the same thing. What God wanted most of all and what He wanted Adam to experience was *fellowship*.

> The Church is going to be to Jesus what Eve would become to Adam, bone of His bone and flesh of His flesh, and thus fulfill His longing for fellowship.

After such a graphic demonstration to Adam of his need for fellowship, God performed a unique operation. He removed one of Adam's ribs and out of it He "built" a woman and placed her in front of him to be his "helper." Adam's response was, "This is the one for whom I have been waiting! This is bone of my bone and flesh of my flesh."

This is a clear picture, in type, of Jesus and the Church. While Jesus slept in the tomb, God took out from His death that which He will build into a Bride for Jesus. The Church is going to be to Jesus what Eve would become to Adam, bone of His bone and flesh of His flesh, and thus fulfill His longing for fellowship.

We come back once again to this tremendous truth that the supreme aim and purpose of God is fellowship with man.

I will now summarize briefly the five distinctive characteristics of Adam as I have described them in this and the previous chapter. They apply to every one of us as descendants of Adam, and they uncover many of the deepest needs in our lives.

- *The method of creation:* Adam's body was molded of clay but then directly in-breathed by the Spirit of Almighty God, thus bringing God and Adam into a face-to-face confrontation with each other. This was the basis for Adam's relationship with God and gave him a capacity for fellowship with God unlike that of any other creature.
- *The special nature of man:* Inwardly Adam was created with a special likeness to God that was spiritual, moral and intellectual. Externally his physical form mirrored the form of the Creator.
- *The purpose of man's creation:* Adam was to exercise authority as God's representative over all the earth.
- *Man's position as an intelligent partner with God:* At a certain point in His relationship with Adam, God stepped aside and said, "Adam, what do you think we should call these animals?" So Adam became responsible for the classification of the animal kingdom.
- *The provision of a mate:* God first provoked in Adam a sense of need for someone with whom to share personal, intimate fellowship. Then He satisfied it by the provision of Eve. This became a pattern of the relationship that God intended to develop between Christ and His Bride, the Church.

In the exercise of his responsibilities, God gave Adam a free will. He could always choose to obey or disobey. Free will is a mockery if there is no choice. After creating

Adam, God did not remain around, like a policeman on duty, following Adam and saying, "Now do this!" or "Don't do that!"

Apparently, God left Adam and Eve for significant periods on their own. Genesis 3:8 describes "the LORD God walking in the garden in the cool of the day"—literally, "the wind of the day." That would be about the time that it was getting a little cool and the evening breeze was beginning to blow. It seems clear that God had not been in the Garden all day. The suggestion is that He used to drop in for a visit and fellowship in the evening.

Although God did not remain permanently present in person in the Garden, He left with Adam one permanent representative, one thing that always represented God, one thing that never departed from him. Do you know what that was? *His Word!* God left Adam a word.

I emphasize this because we have a direct parallel between this situation and the new creation in Christ. When we are created anew in Christ, God does not follow us around like a policeman, saying, "Do this!" or "Don't do that!" He does not wave a big stick at us all the time. But He has left with us one permanent representative of Himself: His Word. In John 14:23, Jesus told Judas Thaddeus: "If anyone loves Me, he will keep My word; and My Father will love him, and We will come to him and make Our home with him."

How then does He come to us? How does He make His abode with us? He comes to us and abides with us *through His Word.* The place that God's Word has in our lives is the place that God Himself has. The same honor and respect that we owe to God, we owe to His Word.

We do not love God more than we love His Word. The test of our relationship to God is our attitude toward His Word.

That was true for Adam. The basis of his relationship to God was his relationship to the Word of God. God did not give Adam, as far as we know, an entire Bible. He gave him two verses: Genesis 2:16–17:

> And the LORD God commanded the man, saying, "Of every tree of the garden you may freely eat; but of the tree of the knowledge of good and evil you shall not eat, for in the day that you eat of it you shall surely die."

That was the Word of the "LORD God." It was the truth. In Genesis 3:4, however, Satan speaks his word: "You will *not* surely die" (emphasis added). That was a lie—Satan's lie. Adam and Eve were confronted by a situation in which they had to make a clear-cut choice between God's truth and Satan's lie. Their tragic error was that they rejected the truth of God's Word and received Satan's lie.

"You can sin and get away with it." That is *the* lie. But the truth is: "In the day that you eat of it you shall surely die." Adam's descendants are still confronted by the same choice that he himself had to make in the Garden. You and I still today must each make our choices. We cannot remain neutral. We each settle our destinies by the way we respond to God's Word.

> The same honor and respect that we owe to God, we owe to His Word.

Note the three successive phases to God's Word as He gave it to Adam. First of all, there is *permission*. God begins with a positive: "You may eat of every tree that is in the Garden except one." Next there is a *prohibition*: "But of the tree of the knowledge of good and evil you shall not eat." Finally, the third phrase is a *warning*: "In the day that you eat of it you shall surely die."

As long as Adam believed and obeyed God's Word, no evil could touch him. Nothing could take away his peace, his life or his blessing. But the moment he rejected God's Word, even though God was not personally present in the Garden at that time, he had rejected God. Let me state this again, because it is one of the great basic lessons of all Scripture: *Your attitude toward God's Word determines your relationship with God.*

Perhaps you have not shaken your fist in God's face and said, "God, I do not want You in my life." However, rejecting or disobeying His Word is as much an act of defiance as shaking your fist in His face. Your attitude to the Word is your attitude toward God.

Notice again the correspondence between the creation described in Genesis and the new creation in Christ. When God created Adam He did not then look around and say, "Now where are We going to put him? What is he going to eat?" Everything Adam needed was perfectly provided in the foreknowledge of God. He placed Adam in a situation where every need was already taken care of—except for the provision of a wife. Adam needed nothing that was not there. There was one condition for remaining in this perfect provision: to believe and obey God's Word.

106

As I understand the New Testament, exactly the same things are true of every person created anew in Christ. When God creates a sinner anew in Christ, He does not then look around and say, "What am I going to do for him? How shall I keep him? What will he live on? How will he find the answers to his problems?"

In the new creation, everything we will ever need is already provided in Christ. Like Adam in the Garden, we are placed into a complete and perfect provision. This is clearly described in 2 Peter 1:2–4:

> Grace and peace be multiplied to you in the knowledge of God and of Jesus our Lord, as His divine power has given to us all things that pertain to life and godliness, through the knowledge of Him who called us by glory and virtue, by which have been given to us exceedingly great and precious promises, that through these you may be partakers of the divine nature, having escaped the corruption that is in the world through lust.

Notice the tense used in this Scripture: God's "divine power *has* given to us"—not *will* give but *has* given to us—"all things that pertain to life and godliness." God does not have to give us anything more. It has all already been given to us in Jesus Christ. It all comes through the knowledge of Christ and it is all contained in the exceeding great and precious promises of His Word.

Adam was created and put into a place of perfect provision. Not one thing was lacking. The only condition for remaining there was believing and obeying God's Word.

Likewise, you and I, re-created in Christ, are put into a complete and perfect provision. Everything we shall ever need, for time and eternity, is already provided. The only condition for remaining in this perfect provision is believing and obeying the Word of God. Adam's critical error was that he did not submit to the authority of God's Word. That is also our great basic error as Christians.

Questions for This Study

1. Man was created to be a _____ and to _____ _____ over _____ the earth.

2. What permanent representative of God do we have in common with Adam, and how does it test our relationship to God?

_____

_____

_____

_____

3. How do you settle your destiny?

_____

_____

4. What has God's divine power given to us, according to 2 Peter 1:2–4, and how do we get it?

_____

_____

_____

_____

_____

Life Application

1. What do you believe your destiny is?

2. What does fellowship with God mean to you and how do you find it?

3. What does it mean for you to have dominion on earth today?

Notes

_____

_____

_____

_____

_____

_____

_____

Memory Verse

Grace and peace be multiplied to you in the knowledge of God and of Jesus our Lord, as His divine power has given to us all things that pertain to life and godliness, through the knowledge of Him who called us by glory and virtue, by which have been given to us exceedingly great and precious promises, that through these you may be partakers of the divine nature, having escaped the corruption that is in the world through lust.

2 Peter 1:2–4

Faith Response

Father, You have provided everything I need for life and godliness in Christ. I choose to live in these gifts. Open the eyes of my understanding to grasp how to live as You would have me live as a true child of God. I believe You want me to enforce and extend Your kingdom here on earth as I lift up and glorify Jesus Christ. Lead me in this, Lord.

7   One Man and His Prayer

Satan's pride and rebellion cost him his place of honor and privilege in the heavenlies. Many Christians assume that he was permanently exiled from the heavenly regions. They speak and pray as if Satan were in hell, but that is not the picture given in Scripture. According to Revelation 20:13–15, as I have mentioned, Death and Hades (Hell) are satanic angels who rule at this time in the lower world to which the unbelieving are consigned at death, together with other creatures who have been in rebellion against their Creator (see 2 Peter 2:4). This would include the angels that had intercourse with human women, as described in Genesis 6:2–4.

Hades is also a title for the area that they rule. But Satan himself is not confined there with them. Ultimately Death and Hades will be cast into the lake of fire together with all the remaining enemies of God.

In Ephesians 2:2, Satan is called the "prince of the power of the air," meaning the satanic ruler of the spiritual region defined as "the air." In Greek, there are two words for *air*: *aither*, associated with the English word *ether*, and *aer*, associated with the English word *air*. The second word, *aer*, denotes the air immediately contiguous with the earth's surface. The first word, *aither*, denotes the higher rarefied atmosphere and is never applied to the air contiguous with the earth's surface.

Significantly, wherever Satan is called "the ruler of the air" it is the word *aer* that is used. In other words, Satan claims dominion over the entire surface of the globe.

In Daniel 10, we are given a glimpse of the activity that goes on amongst angels, both the angels of God and the angels of Satan. Apparently there is ongoing conflict between the angels of God and the forces of Satan that oppose them. It takes place in the area referred to as the mid-heaven.

Daniel's Prayer Is Answered

As chapter 10 opens, we find Daniel mourning and semi-fasting for 21 days. He has been seeking God in deep grief because of the enslavement of his people Israel and the desolation of the city of Jerusalem:

> In those days, I, Daniel, was mourning three full weeks. I ate no pleasant food, no meat or wine came into my mouth, nor did I anoint myself at all, till three whole weeks were fulfilled.
>
> verses 2–3

Daniel is rewarded by a visitation from Gabriel, an archangel of God. As we study Gabriel's visit to Daniel, we need to bear in mind that chapters 10, 11 and 12 of the book of Daniel are a single continuous revelation of events that will bring Israel's history in the present dispensation to a climax.

Gabriel begins his message with words of encouragement:

> Then he said to me, "Do not fear, Daniel, for from the first day that you set your heart to understand, and to humble yourself before your God, your words were heard; and I have come because of your words."
>
> verse 12

Daniel had been praying for 21 days and his prayer was heard the first day. *But the answer only came the twenty-first day.* What was the reason for the delay? The reason is given in verse 13:

> "But the prince of the kingdom of Persia withstood me twenty-one days; and behold, Michael, one of the chief princes [archangels], came to help me, for I had been left alone there with the kings of Persia."

Notice that these events are entirely on the angelic level. The only human being involved is Daniel. The archangel Gabriel is sent from God in answer to the prayer of Daniel to bring him a revelation. Satan, however, knowing the significance of that revelation, releases all his forces in the mid-heaven to prevent the archangel Gabriel from coming to the earth with it.

Gabriel is opposed primarily by the "prince of the kingdom of Persia." This is not a man but a satanic angel charged by Satan with a two-fold task: resisting God's purposes and enforcing Satan's will in the kingdom of Persia.

> It is important to remember that Satan has the earth—its kingdoms, its empires and its governments—assigned to the various angels under him.

It is important to remember that Satan has the earth—its kingdoms, its empires and its governments—assigned to the various angels under him. A similar case applies to our contemporary political situation. We may be sure that Satan has one of his main angels responsible for sowing confusion in Washington, D.C. He has another angel responsible for Beijing and another for Moscow and another for London. If we do not understand these things, we can never become the kind of effective prayer warriors God has called us to be.

The angelic conflict in the heavens between the forces of God and the forces of Satan, recorded in Daniel 10, became so intense that a second archangel, Michael, had to come to the help of Gabriel.

This confrontation between Gabriel and Michael on the one hand and Satan's angels on the other was no little skirmish. It took 21 days for Gabriel to break through the ranks of Satan's angels, who were opposing his descent from God's heaven to the human earth.

What is the activity of angels when they fight one

another? One key word that is used in reference to angels in conflict is *stand* or *take a stand*. In Daniel 10:13, Gabriel says, "The prince of the kingdom of Persia *withstood* me twenty-one days" (emphasis added). This means "took his stand against me."

Again, in Daniel 11:1, the same angel says: "Also in the first year of Darius the Mede, I, even I, *stood up* to confirm and strengthen him" (emphasis added).

These two great archangels, Gabriel and Michael, were united in this task of ministering to Daniel and bringing an answer to his prayer.

Then, in fulfillment of his mission, Gabriel begins to tell Daniel what the future holds:

> "Now I have come to explain to you what will happen to your people in the future, for the vision concerns a time yet to come." . . . So he said, "Do you know why I have come to you? Soon I will return to fight against the prince of Persia, and when I go, the prince of Greece will come; but first I will tell you what is written in the Book of Truth. (No one supports me against them except Michael, your prince.)"
>
> Daniel 10:14, 20–21 NIV

Notice that Michael is called "your prince" in relation to the fact that Daniel was an Israelite. Michael is the archangel who is particularly responsible for enforcing God's purposes for Israel. Look at Daniel 12:1: "At that time Michael shall stand up, the great prince who stands watch over the sons of your people [Israel]."

Whenever Scripture depicts Michael as particularly

active, we may conclude that Israel is center stage on earth.

This is indeed the case here as Gabriel says, in effect, "My battle is not yet won." Then he continues, "When we have dealt with the kings of Persia, the next one to confront us will be the prince of Greece." (The "prince of Greece" is the satanic angel responsible for seeing Satan's will enforced in the empire of Greece.)

Why were Persia and Greece of particular importance at this stage? Because of their relationship to Israel.

Four successive kingdoms were responsible in some measure for the captivity of Israel and held rule over their land and over the city of Jerusalem. These successive kingdoms were Babylon, Persia, Greece and Rome. The focus of prophecy at this stage was the land and people of Israel. Each of these four nations in turn was important because of its historical involvement with Israel.

> God's prophetic clock has started to tick once more.

Then in AD 70 when the Jewish people were dispersed and Israel ceased to exist as a geographical entity, the focus of prophecy changed. In the seventeen or eighteen centuries that followed, biblical prophecy was relevant to very few significant world events. But now that the Jewish people have returned to the land of Israel, prophecy has started to be relevant again. God's prophetic clock has started to tick once more. The scene is being set for the culmination of this age. Daniel 7, 8, 11 and 12 all focus on this period in which we are currently living.

The Role of Intercession

What excites me most about the incidents recorded above is that the ministry of intercession played a decisive role. Heaven did not move until Daniel prayed. Heaven's angels could not get through until Daniel prayed them through.

But that demanded *persistence*. If we are praying a prayer that does not get answered immediately, it may not be because our prayer is not in the will of God. It may be because there is a satanic prince up in the heavenlies standing in the way of the answer. So what do we have to do? Pray him out of the way!

Daniel did not leave the initiative with the enemy. He himself chose the battleground of prayer. When confronted with opposition, he persisted. Sometimes opposition from Satan is one of the best indications that we are praying in the will of God.

We find two complementary elements in Daniel's prayer life. Number one, he had cultivated a life of prayer from his youth. This was so important to him that even the threat of being cast into the lions' den did not deter him. He maintained regular times of prayer throughout the day.

Number two, Daniel did not pray according to his own ideas, but rather for the fulfillment of God's purpose as revealed in Scripture. The LORD God had quickened to him a passage from the prophet Jeremiah:

I, Daniel, understood from the Scriptures, according to the word of the LORD given to Jeremiah the prophet, that the desolation of Jerusalem would last seventy years. So

> I turned to the Lord God and pleaded with him in prayer
> and petition, in fasting, and in sackcloth and ashes.
>
> Daniel 9:2–3 NIV

Any believer who gives himself to the ministry of intercession needs to be a diligent student of biblical prophecy because this is the primary basis of all truly effective prayer. An overall outline of the outworking of God's purposes revealed in prophecy is given by Jesus Himself in Matthew 24 and 25. Any believer who gives himself to prayer along this line should make a diligent study of the picture of the end time that Jesus Himself gave in these two chapters.

> Any believer who gives himself to the ministry of intercession needs to be a diligent student of biblical prophecy because this is the primary basis of all truly effective prayer.

A serious problem with many believers is that we underestimate our own influence and potential. Yet in a certain sense, the universe revolves around us. When we pray, heaven moves. If we hold out in prayer, heaven's purposes are fulfilled. If we give up praying, the purposes of God are frustrated.

One fact of vital importance for our prayer life emerges from the incidents related above. Unfortunately, however, few Christians have come to grips with it. The fact is this: *In order to ascend from earth to the throne of God's authority, our prayers may have to pass through a territory occupied by our enemy*. This was obviously true of Daniel's prayers recorded above. They were being opposed by a satanic prince in the heavenlies called "the prince of Persia." In the end, however, Daniel's persistent prayer caused this satanic prince to yield. The effectiveness of Daniel's praying was not manifest in the natural realm. He was not dealing with human beings; he was dispelling satanic forces in the heavenlies that were opposing God's purposes.

Challenged by Daniel's example, we need to ask certain questions before we give ourselves to prayer:

Are my prayers based on Scripture or are they just the expression of my own wishful thinking?

Do I pray the kind of aggressive, irresistible prayers that will reach God's throne?

When I pray, am I prepared to deal with satanic spiritual forces in a heavenly realm and not merely with situations on a purely human level?

I was talking once to a group of Methodists on the subject of prayer, and I remarked, "Some people read prayers, some people say prayers and some people pray."

Of course, this provoked some questions. "What's the difference?" they asked.

"Well," I replied, "a person who's really praying doesn't just read a prayer or say a prayer, but he becomes his own prayer."

I went on to explain that this was true of David when he was under tremendous pressure, as recorded in Psalm 109:3–4: "They have also surrounded me with words of hatred, and fought against me without a cause. In return for my love they are my accusers, *but I give myself to prayer*" (emphasis added).

The English translation reads, "I give myself to prayer." But the translators have inserted words not included in the original Hebrew. What David actually said was, "But I prayer." In other words, "I became my own prayer."

Elijah on Mount Carmel provides us with a picture of this kind of prayer:

> And Elijah went up to the top of Carmel; then he bowed down on the ground, and put his face between his knees, and said to his servant, "Go up now, look toward the sea." So he went up and looked, and said, "There is nothing." And seven times he said, "Go again." Then it came to pass the seventh time, that he said, "There is a cloud, as small as a man's hand, rising out of the sea!" So he said, "Go up, say to Ahab, 'Prepare your chariot, and go down before the rain stops you.'"
>
> 1 Kings 18:42–44

At this point Elijah did not merely say a prayer, *he became his own prayer*. His whole body became an instrument that responded to the Spirit of God moving within him, and releasing the supernatural power of God through him.

But in Hebrews 5:7 there is one yet greater pattern of this kind of prayer as the writer describes Jesus:

> Who, in the days of His flesh, when He had offered up prayers and supplications, with vehement cries and tears to Him who was able to save Him from death, and was heard because of His godly fear.

Elijah on Mount Carmel and Jesus in Gethsemane became vehicles of a supernatural power that broke through all satanic opposition and released the purposes of God.

For effective prayer, there are two things we need: *authority* and *power.* Authority is a legal concept. To have authority we must have confidence that we have fulfilled all the legal requirements. Once we have fulfilled these, praying in the name of Jesus sets the seal of His authority upon our prayer. He Himself stressed continually: "If you ask anything *in My name,* I will do it." Praying such a prayer is like sending a registered letter. No one can tamper with it or stop it. It is guaranteed to reach its destination.

> For effective prayer, there are two things we need: **authority** and **power.**

As Christians in the world today, we may expect to be confronted by situations in which nothing less than the kind of prayer demonstrated by Elijah and by Jesus will bring victory. Frequently it will express itself in powerful, uninhibited praise. Our prayers will need to be supernaturally empowered to penetrate the area in the mid-heaven where Satan seeks to oppose us.

An illustration is provided by the technique by which NASA engineers launch a shuttle into space.

They attach a rocket booster to the shuttle, and this, when activated, provides the energy needed to project the shuttle above the atmosphere of the earth. But the release of the rocket is accompanied by an almost blinding flash and then a loud sustained roar during the shuttle's ascent through the earth's atmosphere. Once it has reached a certain altitude, it will carry on under its own momentum. There is no way to release a rocket, however, without a powerful impact on the senses.

In a similar way, the release of the power needed to project our prayers through the mid-heaven makes a powerful impact upon the senses. Sometimes we have the impression that prayer must be solemn and dignified. But there is nothing solemn or dignified about the release of a rocket.

Spiritual conflict will inevitably test our character. Daniel provides us with three challenging examples.

First, Daniel's prayer *cost him something*. By going on a partial fast for three weeks, he sacrificed his own carnal pleasure.

Second, he *did not yield* to discouragement. In spite of the fact that there was no tangible evidence that God was hearing his prayer and that a response was on the way, he continued to pour out his heart before his God.

Third, because of Daniel's *courage and persistence* the subsequent outworking of God's purposes for Israel was released. It was his prayer life that gave him his unique position in the history of his people.

The following are important lessons that we can learn from Daniel's prayer life:

From his youth, Daniel's prayer was a way of life, not a religious activity. He reserved a set time and place each day that he gave exclusively to prayer.

Daniel did not improvise his own prayer. The original impulse to pray came from the prophetic Scriptures. He prayed for the fulfillment of God's will for His people as revealed in Scripture.

Daniel's prayer demanded self-denial and was accompanied by fasting. In the Sermon on the Mount, Jesus said to His disciples, "*When* you pray . . . *when* you fast. . . ." He did not say, "*If* you pray" or "*if* you fast." He took it for granted that His disciples would practice both prayer and fasting. There are times when prayer alone is not sufficient. It needs to be supernaturally empowered by fasting.

Daniel was totally committed to praying. As I mentioned earlier, even the threat of being cast into the lions' den did not cause him to waver.

This brings out one fact often neglected by Christians during times of spiritual conflict: *Effective praying tests our character. It demands single-hearted commitment.*

Praying as he did projected Daniel into a level of activity far above that of earth. The last three chapters of the book of Daniel contain a total of 78 verses. Daniel himself is the only human being involved. The other beings depicted are angels.

Let us turn our focus to these amazing creatures.

Questions for This Study

1. Drawing from the confrontation between Gabriel and the prince of the kingdom of Persia, where does Satan have various angels assigned? _____

_____, _____ and _____

2. What is a serious problem with many believers?

_____

3. What two things are needed for effective prayer?

_____ and _____

4. What fact is often neglected during times of spiritual conflict?

_____

_____

_____

Life Application

1. What has this study of Daniel and Elijah done to enlarge your understanding of your responsibility to pray?

2. How can you position yourself to become more effective in understanding prophecy and fulfilling your part in intercession?

3. Why does effective praying test your character?

Notes

_____

_____

_____

_____

_____

_____

Memory Verse

The effective, fervent prayer of a righteous man avails much.

James 5:16b

Faith Response

Father, I receive this greater understanding and revelation on effective praying. I see my need to pray in line with Your heart and Word so my prayers bring about change in this world. I want prayers that will advance the realm of Your Kingdom so Your influence and dominion rule here.

8 Angelic Beings

The Scriptures contain many references to angels. It is surprising, therefore, that this subject is often neglected by preachers. Yet angels play a very significant role in the unfolding of God's purposes.

In Psalm 104, David defines the nature of angels: They are *spirits*. God "makes His angels spirits" (verse 4).

Now, we know that man also has a spirit within him. In 1 Thessalonians 5:23, Paul prays for the Christians: "May the God of peace Himself sanctify you *completely*; and may your whole *spirit, soul, and body* be preserved blameless" (emphasis added). Our complete personality is made up of these three elements: spirit, soul and body.

Scripture reveals that spirit-beings are eternal. The spirit in each one of us will never cease to exist. Thus, both men and angels are confronted with this solemn realization: *They will never cease to exist.* Those who refuse God's mercy are doomed to spend eternity in a lake of fire to which there is no end and no exit.

The Divine "Angel"

First and foremost in our study of angelic beings, we need to understand that God Himself often appeared to men as an "Angel" (note the capital *A*). For instance, this divine Angel appeared to Hagar, the concubine of Abraham, when she was fleeing from Sarah: "The Angel of the LORD said to her [Hagar], 'Return to your mistress, and submit yourself under her hand'" (Genesis 16:9).

> First and foremost in our study of angelic beings, we need to understand that God Himself often appeared to men as an "Angel."

Then He added: "I will multiply your descendants exceedingly, so that they shall not be counted for multitude" (verse 10).

Later on, the Angel said again: "Arise, lift up the lad and hold him with your hand, for I will make him a great nation" (21:18).

Only God Himself, manifested in the person of the Angel, could make such promises as these: "I will multiply his descendants exceedingly," and "I will make him a great nation."

This Angel also appeared to Moses: "And the Angel of the LORD appeared to him in a flame of fire from the midst of a bush" (Exodus 3:2).

Two verses later, this same Angel is specifically called "God": "God called to him from the midst of the bush" (verse 4).

Another example is the appearance of the Angel to Gideon:

> And the Angel of the LORD appeared to him, and said to him, "The LORD is with you, you mighty man of valor!" Gideon said to Him, "O my lord, if the LORD is with us, why then has all this happened to us? And where are all His miracles which our fathers told us about . . . ?"
>
> Judges 6:12–13

In the exchange that follows, this Angel is actually called "the LORD," which, as we have seen, is the accepted way to render in English the sacred name of four Hebrew letters usually translated "Jehovah" or "Yahweh." "Then *the LORD turned to him* and said, 'Go in this might of yours, and you shall save Israel from the hand of the Midianites. Have I not sent you?'" (verse 14, emphasis added).

The phrase *the LORD turned to him* indicates that there was direct, face-to-face confrontation between Yahweh and Gideon. They were conversing together as person to person.

Later on (see Judges 13:3–23) the same Angel appeared to the parents of Samson: "the Angel of God came to the woman" (verse 9), and in the following verse: "The woman . . . said to him, 'Look, the *Man* . . . has just now appeared to me'" (verse 10, emphasis added).

In verse 22, Manoah, Samson's father, says: "We shall surely die, because we have seen God!"

So, this Person who appeared to the parents of Samson was a "Man," an Angel (a messenger from God) and also God Himself.

Who was this mysterious Person? Out of my own spiritual experience, I have no question as to His identity. He was the same Person who later was manifested in history as Jesus of Nazareth. Jesus combined in Himself all the three natures: God, an Angel (messenger) and a Man.

At least two other appearances of this divine Angel are recorded in Israel's history. Numbers 22 records how Balak, king of Moab, sent for the soothsayer, Balaam, to curse Israel. But while Balaam was on his way to do this, "the LORD opened Balaam's eyes, and he saw the Angel of the LORD standing in the way with His drawn sword in His hand; and he bowed his head and fell flat on his face" (verse 31). By this response Balaam acknowledged that he was in the presence of God.

After this confrontation, the Angel released Balaam to continue his journey, but strictly warned him: "Only the word that I speak to you, that you shall speak" (verse 35). The result was that Balaam gave forth three successive and glorious prophecies unfolding God's destiny for His people Israel.

Later on in Israel's history, the southern kingdom of Judah was attacked by Assyria and the city of Jerusalem was besieged. In answer to the prayer of King Hezekiah, however, "the angel [or Angel] of the LORD went out, and killed in the camp of the Assyrians one hundred and eighty-five thousand; and when people arose early in the morning, there were the corpses—all dead" (2 Kings 19:35). That certainly was an awesome demonstration of God's power working through the Angel.

Physical Features of Angels

Various passages of Scripture also describe angels who are not divine but created beings.

These heavenly beings are spirits, but they are equipped with bodies that enable them to carry out their various functions. In many cases, their bodies are represented as having wings. Angels with different functions differ in the number of their wings.

In Solomon's Temple, for instance, cherubs are represented as having two wings. (The plural form of *cherub* in Hebrew is *cherubim*.) "For the cherubim spread their two wings over the place of the ark, and the cherubim overshadowed the ark and its poles" (1 Kings 8:7).

It is of interest that *cherub* is the modern Hebrew word for *cabbage*. What is the association? Perhaps it is because the way that the wings of a cherub are attached to its body is similar to the way a cabbage leaf grows from its stalk.

Here are further details of the cherubs depicted in the Most Holy Place of the Temple:

> Various passages of Scripture also describe angels who are not divine but created beings.

The wings of the cherubim were twenty cubits in overall length: one wing of the one cherub was five cubits, touching the wall of the room, and the other wing was five cubits, touching the wing of the other cherub; one wing of the other cherub was five cubits, touching the wall of the room, and the other wing also was five cubits, touching the wing of the other cherub. The wings of these cherubim spanned twenty cubits overall. They stood on their feet, and they faced inward.

2 Chronicles 3:11–13

These cherubs were awesome figures. Five cubits is seven and a half feet. That brings the total wingspan of each cherub to fifteen feet.

Ezekiel 1:5–11 gives a detailed description of cherubs who have four wings called "living creatures":

And this was their appearance: they had the likeness of a man. Each one had four faces, and each one had four wings. Their legs were straight, and the soles of their feet were like the soles of calves' feet. They sparkled like the color of burnished bronze. The hands of a man were under their wings on their four sides; and each of the four had faces and wings. Their wings touched one another. The creatures [cherubs] did not turn when they went, but each one went straight forward.

As for the likeness of their faces, each had the face of a man; each of the four had the face of a lion on the right side, each of the four had the face of an ox on the left side, and each of the four had the face of an eagle. Thus were their faces. Their wings were stretched upward; two wings of each one touched one another, and two covered their bodies.

Another kind of angelic being called *seraph* is described in Isaiah 6. *Seraph* is directly connected with the Hebrew word for *fire*. These were burning, fiery creatures who guarded the approach to the Lord of hosts. Anybody who desired access to Him had to pass through the fire.

Each of the seraphim had six wings: "Above it [the throne of the LORD] stood seraphim; each one had six wings: with two he covered his face, with two he covered his feet, and with two he flew" (verse 2).

Covering the face and covering the feet were acts of worship. The remaining two wings were used for flying, which was service. In heaven there is twice as much emphasis on worship as on service. Should not the proportion be the same here on earth?

"And one cried to another and said: 'Holy, holy, holy is the LORD of hosts; the whole earth is full of His glory!'" (verse 3). The triple utterance by the seraphim of the word *holy* was their response to the revelation of a triune God, that is, one God in three Persons.

Later, we will look at some passages in Scripture that refer to angels engaged in war. Not one speaks of angels being killed. To speak of a "dead angel" would seem to be a contradiction in terms.

In 1 Corinthians 15:50, Paul speaks of a category of beings who have "flesh and blood." His use of this phrase suggests that he is contrasting this type of being with those who have flesh but no blood. My impression is that the first being to have both flesh and blood was Adam. The ultimate purpose was that Jesus, as "the last Adam," might offer His blood as the final, all-sufficient sacrifice for the sin of the whole Adamic race.

The Ministry of Angels

What purposes do the angels serve?

Angels are not merely spirits but they are *ministering* spirits, sent forth by God to serve His people and His purposes: "Are they not all *ministering* spirits sent forth to minister for those who will inherit salvation?" (Hebrews 1:14, emphasis added). The Bible offers many accounts of angels sent out to minister to members of the Adamic race in their times of need.

As already stated, the Greek word used in the New Testament for *angel* is *angelos,* which means "a messenger." The Hebrew word used in the Old Testament for *angel* is *malach,* meaning "servant." Angels therefore are *servant messengers* sent forth with special tasks. Here are some of them.

Bring Revelations

One important function assigned to angels at times was to bring revelations that were actually recorded as Scripture. For example, the messages of the first six chapters of the prophet Zechariah were brought to him by angels. Various sections of the book of Daniel were given by angels.

But the most significant of all is the book of Revelation, which is the culmination of all Scripture: "Then he said to me, 'These words are faithful and true.' And the Lord God of the holy prophets *sent His angel* to show His servants the things which must shortly take place" (22:6, emphasis added). This indicates that the whole content of the book of Revelation was communicated to John by an angel.

Further on in this same chapter Jesus Himself clearly states: "I, Jesus, *have sent My angel* to testify to you these things in the churches" (verse 16, emphasis added).

Deliver Other Messages

The Bible also contains examples of angels sent from God with various messages for individuals. For instance, Zacharias, while serving as a priest in the Temple, received a message from an angel foretelling the birth of John the Baptist (see Luke 1:11–25). Later the archangel Gabriel appeared to the virgin Mary and announced that she would conceive a Son, who was to be called Jesus (Savior) (see Luke 1:26–38).

At the climax of the ministry of Jesus, as He was praying in the Garden of Gethsemane, an angel appeared to Him strengthening Him for the ordeal that lay ahead: "Then an angel appeared to Him from heaven, strengthening Him" (Luke 22:43).

Serve the Saints on Earth

In Luke 16:19–31, Jesus describes the death of the beggar named Lazarus and briefly lifts the veil over the events that followed: "So it was that the beggar died, and was carried by the angels to Abraham's bosom" (verse 22).

I am always gripped by the fact that a company of angels escorted Lazarus. Surely one angel could have carried that emaciated form into God's presence. But God honored him with an escort. His values are so different from ours. "He raises the poor from the dust and lifts the beggar from the ash heap, to set them among princes and make them inherit the throne of glory" (1 Samuel 2:8).

On the other hand, Jesus warns us: "For what is highly esteemed among men is an abomination in the sight of God" (Luke 16:15). May God preserve us from giving our lives to things that are an abomination to Him!

Provide Protection

Another ministry of angels is to rescue God's servants from situations of danger. There are many examples of this in Scripture. Daniel 3:19–25 records how Shadrach, Meshach and Abed-Nego refused to honor Nebuchadnezzar's god and were cast into a fiery furnace, which should have meant instant death. But a fourth unnamed being—by his presence—preserved them from all harm and they came out to glorify God. Undoubtedly, that fourth person was an angelic being.

Later Daniel refused to renege on his commitment to pray to the God of Israel for the city of Jerusalem and, as a consequence, he was thrown into the lions' den (see Daniel 6:10–23). However, Daniel spent a more restful night with the lions than King Darius in his palace. The next morning, Daniel reassured the king: "My God sent His angel and shut the lions' mouths, so that they have not hurt me" (verse 22).

The New Testament records similar interventions by angels for God's people when imprisoned. Acts 5:17–28 recounts how the apostles were imprisoned for preaching the Gospel. But an angel of the Lord supernaturally opened the prison doors, led them out and closed the doors securely behind them. Then he instructed the apostles to go on teaching the people in the Temple.

Further on, Acts 12:4–19 relates how Peter was imprisoned awaiting execution. But an angel of the Lord roused him from sleep, released his shackles and led him safely out of the prison. At this point Peter realized that this was not a dream and he said: "Now I know for certain that the Lord has sent His angel, and has delivered me from the hand of Herod and from all the expectation of the Jewish people" (verse 11).

Old and New Testaments alike assure us that God will, at times, intervene through angels on behalf of His servants in situations of danger and will deliver them.

> Old and New Testaments alike assure us that God will, at times, intervene through angels on behalf of His servants in situations of danger and will deliver them.

Intervene Politically

Another extremely important ministry of angels is to intervene in the political arena either by helping to raise up leaders or by setting them aside—according to God's directives. Angels may release their supernatural power in support of leaders who are committed to do God's will, even though these leaders may not actually be serving Him.

An outstanding example is provided by the rise to power of Darius the Mede as described in Daniel 11:1: "Also in the first year of Darius the Mede, I [the angel speaking], even I, stood up to confirm and strengthen him."

Darius was a king of Persia who followed Cyrus and extended the Persian Empire in various directions. He helped to implement the decree of his predecessor, Cyrus, that had opened the way for the Jews to return to their land and to the city of Jerusalem.

The return of the Jews to Jerusalem was an integral and essential part of the historical outworking of God's purposes. To bring this about, God released angelic forces in the heavenlies.

However, the effect of angelic intervention in the processes of history may be negative rather than positive for those involved. For instance, in Acts 12:20–23 King Herod had made an arrogant speech to the people of Tyre and Sidon in which he accepted honor as a god. God's reaction to this was immediate: "An angel of the Lord struck him, because he did not give glory to God. And he was eaten by worms and died" (verse 23). There was a pointed contrast between the honor Herod accepted and the way he died.

Rescue in Time of Need

Not all angelic intervention, however, is directed to producing major historical changes. Angels quite often are sent to help very ordinary people dealing with situations beyond their control.

The story of my first wife, Lydia, is a good example. In 1929, when Lydia was living on her own in Jerusalem, she was seeking to carry a sickly little Jewish baby girl named Tikva away from a street riot that had broken out around her house. The following is an excerpt from my book *Appointment in Jerusalem,* recounting the drama:

Every hundred yards or so I [Lydia] came to a barricade of rocks and other debris piled across the street. Painfully I half climbed, half scrambled over them, still holding Tikva on my shoulders.

After about half a mile I came to a barricade, two or three feet higher than the rest, that marked the line of division between the Jewish and Arab zones. I began to scramble over, but halfway across, my foot slipped on a loose stone and with a rush of rubble I slid down to the bottom again, almost losing Tikva from my shoulders. Realizing that my strength was giving out, I set Tikva down on the ground and sat beside her on a rock. By myself, I felt sure, I could climb over somehow. But how to get Tikva over?

Suddenly I had the uncanny impression that I was no longer by myself. Every muscle in my body tensed. Turning quickly, I was confronted by a young man standing in the road a few feet from me. A scream rose to my lips, but before I could utter it, the young man had picked Tikva up and placed her on his shoulders, in the same position in which I had been carrying her. Then, without apparent effort, he climbed the barricade. Relieved of the burden of Tikva, I succeeded in scrambling over after him.

As soon as I was over, the young man set off along the road—Tikva still on his shoulders and myself following a few feet behind. Still trying to grasp what was happening, I looked more closely at the young man. He was about six feet tall, wearing a dark suit of European cut. Certainly he was not an Arab. He might be Jewish. Where had he come from? How had he appeared so suddenly at my side?

The thing that surprised me most was Tikva's behavior. Normally, if a stranger tried to pick her up, she would start to cry. But I had not heard one murmur from her since the young man picked her up. She was riding just as contentedly on his shoulders as she would have done on mine. Indeed, she seemed to be enjoying herself!

For nearly half a mile the young man strode ahead. He never hesitated as to which road to follow, but took the most direct route to Musrara. Each time we came to a barricade, he climbed it ahead of me, then waited on the other side long enough to make sure that I was safely over. Finally he came to a halt directly in front of Miss Ratcliffe's house, set Tikva down on the street, turned around and started back along the way by which we had come. During our whole encounter he had not spoken a single word, either of greeting or of parting. In a minute he was out of sight. . . .

"However did you get here?" Miss Ratcliffe persisted. . . . I described the journey and the young man who had come to my aid. . . .

"God has answered our prayers! We asked Him to send an angel to protect you, and surely that is what He did!"

In my own first contact with born-again Christians, I was frequently a guest with a family that kept a boardinghouse in Scarborough in Yorkshire. They had an unmarried daughter in her late twenties who might have been described as "simple." One of her domestic chores was to carry the rubbish out of the back door to a side street. From time to time, a man would be waiting for her. He was very well dressed with a bowler hat and a fancy waistcoat with a gold watch chain. He would hand her a certain sum of money, which always exactly covered some bill that needed to be paid. This went on for a long period.

Then one day as he handed her the money he said, "From now on you won't be needing any more," which proved true. By that time, the family income had risen to a level where it covered all their immediate needs.

These are just two of the people I have encountered over the years who have had some kind of contact with angels. I mean a contact that they were *aware of.* We may be sure that these usually invisible hosts are serving God day and night in our midst.

Questions for This Study

1. Often _____ _____ appeared to men and women as an "Angel."

2. Angels have appeared in different forms—to Moses in a _____ _____ _____; to Samson's parents as a _____.

3. Angels are _____ _____ sent forth with special tasks.

4. What are some of the purposes angels serve?

_____

_____

_____

_____

_____

_____

Life Application

1. How many ways and forms can you list from Scripture in which angels ministered on earth?

2. How can you be sure there are angels watching over you?

Notes

_____

_____

_____

_____

_____

_____

_____

Memory Verse

The angel of the LORD encamps all around those who fear Him, and delivers them.

Psalm 34:7

Faith Response

Thank You, Father, for the angels here ministering to me, watching over me to help and protect. You are faithful, so I know they are faithful. Though I do not see them, I believe they are here—these beings who have been with You since creation, watching over mankind, hearkening to Your Word. Give me wisdom in my interactions so that Your Kingdom may be enlarged and enforced.

9   Angels at War

The message and the ministry of Jesus divide all who hear into one or the other of two categories: those who believe and obey or those who reject and rebel. This cleavage between the obedient and the rebellious divides not only human beings but also angels into two categories: those who submit to the Lordship of Jesus and those who reject Him and rebel.

The Bible gives various examples of angels who are obedient to God and at war with angels in rebellion against God. In the events described in the book of Daniel, angels play a decisive role. One other portion of Scripture that gives prominence to angels is the book of Revelation. To understand the message of these two books, it is important to appreciate the part played by angels in spiritual warfare.

Certain angels have specific areas of responsibility allotted to them. This is true both for the angels of God and for the angels of Satan. For example, Michael is described to Daniel as "the great prince who stands watch over the sons of your people" (Daniel 12:1).

Daniel's people are, of course, the nation of Israel. Michael's responsibility for Israel continued even after they were exiled from their land and still continues to this day. As I noted in the last chapter, whenever Scripture focuses on the ministry of the archangel Michael, we may safely conclude that Israel is center stage in the events of history on earth.

We have also noted that Satan has angels to whom he has allotted certain areas of responsibility. You will recall that Daniel 10:13 refers to "the prince of the kingdom of Persia" who was a satanic angel assigned by Satan to enforce his purposes in the nation of Persia.

At times, this brings the angels of God and of Satan into direct conflict with each other. In this context, one characteristic expression that is applied to angels is "stand up." For instance, in Daniel 11:1 the angel communicating with Daniel says: "Also, in the first year of Darius the Mede, I [the angel speaking], even I, *stood up* to confirm and strengthen him" (emphasis added).

Also in the next chapter we read: "At that time Michael *shall stand up*, the great prince who stands watch over the sons of your people. . . . And at that time your people shall be delivered" (12:1, emphasis added).

We might perhaps render the phrase *stand up* alternatively as *take a stand*. In certain situations God's angels take their stand, that is, they affirm the authority that God has committed to them over a certain territory.

These angelic conflicts are no small skirmishes. The conflict between Gabriel and the angels opposing him lasted 21 days. What weapons did they employ? I cannot find any detailed description in Scripture, but my impression is that God's angels do at least three things:

They make proclamations.
They offer praise.
They worship.

It goes without saying that God's people, as well as His angels, are called to use these types of warfare.

Making proclamation is a form of spiritual warfare that is, unfortunately, very little understood in most Christian circles today. Its effect is to release the authority of God's Word into a situation. It may be a situation in our personal lives, or it may be a political situation. Whatever the situation may be, there is no more effective way to release the power of God than by making an appropriate proclamation. I will return to the subject of proclamation in a moment.

Proclamation in turn should be followed by *praise*. If we really believe the things we have proclaimed, then our logical response would be to offer praise without necessarily waiting to see their fulfillment.

> If we really believe the things we have proclaimed, then our logical response would be to offer praise without necessarily waiting to see their fulfillment.

Praise in turn leads naturally into *worship*, where we are no longer conscious of the problems we have been facing but are simply taken up with God Himself. True worship has no goal beyond God, but He Himself is all-sufficient.

Warfare by proclamation, perhaps the least understood of the three types of warfare, is well illustrated by the way that Joshua led Israel into their inheritance in Canaan. The first satanic stronghold that held out against them was the city of Jericho. To have made a direct assault upon those well-defended walls would have cost many casualties. But God showed Joshua a different strategy: *united proclamation by God's people*. This was the weapon that brought down the walls of Jericho without a single casualty to Israel.

If we picture God's angels making proclamations, we might well ask, What kind of proclamation would be appropriate for them to make? I suggest that the essence of all effective proclamation is to quote God's own Word back to Him.

One of the most hotly contested issues at the present time is the right to the land of Israel. An appropriate proclamation, therefore, for the angel Gabriel to make in this connection could be taken from the words of Moses in Exodus 32:13:

> "Remember Abraham, Isaac, and Israel, Your servants, to whom You swore by Your own self, and said to them, 'I will multiply your descendants as the stars of heaven; and *all this land that I have spoken of I give to your descendants, and they shall inherit it forever.*'"
>
> emphasis added

Alternatively, Gabriel could remind the Lord of His own promises made to Jerusalem: "Nevertheless I will remember My covenant with you in the days of your youth, and I will establish an everlasting covenant with you" (Ezekiel 16:60).

He could declare that the promise of the upbuilding of Jerusalem is closely related to Jesus' return: "For the LORD shall build up Zion; He shall appear in His glory" (Psalm 102:16).

Or he could state that God has also promised an eternal future to Jerusalem: "But Judah shall abide forever, and Jerusalem from generation to generation" (Joel 3:20).

These are examples of positive, scriptural proclamations. But proclamation is a two-edged sword. It can be used either for or against God. Satan well understands the power of proclamation, and he sees to it that humanity is bombarded with proclamations from sources under his control.

One such source is Islam, which derives much of its power from the proclamations that it regularly makes, both negative and positive. For instance, around the outside of the Dome of the Rock in Jerusalem, situated on what was previously the site of the Temple, a proclamation written in Arabic deliberately rejects the claims of Jesus: "God has no need of a Son."

Furthermore, five times a day, every day, from every Muslim mosque in the world, the following proclamation goes forth: "There is no God but Allah and Muhammad is his prophet." This proclamation has been going out five times a day for more than 1,400 years. One does not need a calculator to ascertain that over the last fourteen centuries this proclamation has gone out billions of times.

The area of the world regularly covered by this proclamation has been the Middle East. This explains why there is such a tremendously strong antichrist power over this area. It is, in fact, the primary reason why this section of humanity has been so strongly resistant to the claims of Jesus. It is also compelling evidence of the power of proclamation, but unfortunately in this case, it is power for evil rather than for good.

Certain Western nations that are committed to religious liberty are permitting great numbers of Muslim mosques to be established within their jurisdictions. This is particularly true of Britain, where new mosques are constantly being established.

Every new mosque thus established becomes a channel for the standard Islamic proclamations. Secular rulers do not understand the spiritual impact that these multiplied proclamations have upon their people. British Bible teacher David Pawson has predicted that Britain will shortly become an Islamic Republic.

> In the mouth of God's servants, the making of positive proclamations is one of the most powerful weapons that He has given to His people.

In the mouth of God's servants, however, the making of positive proclamations is one of the most powerful weapons that He has given to His people. It is the Holy Spirit Himself who gives us the boldness to make such proclamations:

The Spirit of the Lord God is upon Me,
Because the Lord has anointed Me
To preach good tidings to the poor;
He has sent Me to heal the brokenhearted,
To *proclaim* liberty to the captives,
And the opening of the prison to those who are
    bound;
To *proclaim* the acceptable year of the Lord,
And the day of vengeance of our God.

Isaiah 61:1–2, emphasis added

As God's servants, we have much yet to learn about the power of proclamation, praise and worship. We are often so slow to give Him the glory that is His due. In a vision of my mind I look forward to a day when all those who have been blessed by God will respond by giving Him the glory due to Him. From every continent and island loud and jubilant songs of praise and thanksgiving will be ascending to heaven. I do believe that we cannot calculate the overall impact of such proclamations. Once the earth is touched by the glory of God in this way, it will never remain the same.

Questions for This Study

1. When God's angels stand up (or take a stand), what is it they are affirming?

2. What is the effect of making a proclamation?

3. What are the three forms of spiritual warfare that God's people and His angels are called to use?

(a) _____

(b) _____

(c) _____

4. Give two examples of angels (either of God or of Satan) with positions of specific oversight:

(a) _____

(b) _____

Life Application

1. Using Scripture, compose a proclamation to use concerning an area of spiritual warfare in which you are now or can be involved.

2. Seek the Lord for a proclamation to pray and proclaim over your life or family, and use it daily for the length of time God indicates to you.

Notes

_____

_____

_____

_____

_____

Memory Verse

That the sharing of your faith may become effective by the acknowledgment of every good thing which is in you in Christ Jesus.

Philemon 1:6

Faith Response

Father, may the communication of my faith become effective as I acknowledge every good thing that is in me in Christ Jesus. I thank You for redeeming me by the blood of Jesus. I am more than a conqueror through Christ Jesus, and I can do all things through Him who strengthens me. You will always cause me to triumph, manifesting through me a sweet aroma of the knowledge of Him in every place. I praise You, Father, and thank You, Jesus!

10   Now Salvation Has Come!

The twelfth chapter of the book of Revelation depicts perhaps the greatest victory that God's people will have gained since Jesus won His lonely battle with evil on the hill of Golgotha.

This chapter depicts war on two planes as Satan confronts God's people with a double challenge. In the heavenlies, Satan and his angels oppose Michael and his angels. On earth, Satan pours out a stream of blasphemous accusations against Christians, challenging their claim to have been justified (rendered righteous) through their faith in Christ, accusing them before God day and night.

In response, as servants of Christ, we are expected to make full use of the spiritual weapons that God has provided for us. But they become effective only as we operate out of unity. It is significant that the victory recorded here comes to God's people only when they are united in heaven and on earth, opposing Satan together. History reveals that Satan's most effective tactic, and the one he relies on more than any other, is to bring division within the ranks of the people of God.

As this age draws to a close, the spiritual conflict between the forces of God and the forces of Satan becomes more intense and extends throughout the universe. To understand what this conflict requires of us on earth, we need to ask ourselves: *Why is Satan leveling accusations against us? What is his purpose?*

> As servants of Christ, we are expected to make full use of the spiritual weapons that God has provided for us.

Obviously his purpose is to prove us *guilty.* In all his dealings, Satan's primary weapon is guilt. If he succeeds in proving his charges against us, then we no longer qualify to receive God's blessings. Left to ourselves, we are no match in spiritual warfare with Satan.

Scripture assures us, however, that God has given us the spiritual weapons that are needed for this spiritual warfare and they are guaranteed to bring total victory if used correctly.

> For though we walk in the flesh, we do not war according to the flesh. For the weapons of our warfare are not carnal but mighty in God for pulling down strongholds, casting down arguments and every high thing that exalts itself against the knowledge of God, bringing every thought into captivity to the obedience of Christ.
>
> 2 Corinthians 10:3–5

God has given us weapons that are appropriate to our warfare. Our warfare is not carnal—it is not in the physical or material realm. Therefore, our weapons likewise are not carnal or material; they are not bullets or guns, tanks or airplanes. They are spiritual weapons for spiritual warfare.

In verse 5, the apostle Paul tells us that through these weapons we can cast down "every high thing that exalts itself against the knowledge of God." That is an amazing statement! We could read it many times without fully appreciating what it says. But God is telling us that through the weapons that He has committed to us, we can become His agents to cast down the one supremely high thing that opposes God's Kingdom: *Satan's kingdom in the heavenlies.*

Revelation 12:7–9 depicts a war in heaven in which Michael and his angels are opposing the devil and his angels:

> And war broke out in heaven: Michael and his angels fought with the dragon [Satan]; and the dragon and his angels fought, but they did not prevail, nor was a place found for them in heaven any longer. So the great dragon was cast out, that serpent of old, called the Devil and Satan, who deceives the whole world; he was cast to the earth, and his angels were cast out with him.

As I was pondering the conflict described above, I had a vivid mental picture of myself in heaven. All the heavenly hosts of God encircled His throne with a symphony of praise. Then, absolute silence. Suddenly, the songs of Christians worshiping on earth began to rise up. By contrast with the voices of angels, they sounded pathetic in their weakness. Yet I felt they were making an essential contribution to the purposes of God.

For some reason, my mind carried me back to the five years that I spent in East Africa. Once again I heard the words of a Christian chorus that we used to sing in Swahili: *Nguvu za sheitani zimeshindwa,* meaning, "The power of Satan has been conquered."

After awhile, I heard the sound of robes rustling, but I could see no visible change in the scene before my eyes. The rustling grew louder and louder. Suddenly I realized that the rustling sound proceeded from the garments of Satan's angels vacating their abode in heaven.

Then another sound broke in upon my ears—a loud, sustained roar. It began somewhere on the level of heaven but gradually spiraled downward to the level of earth. At first it seemed to express savage rage, but as it descended lower and lower, its tone gradually changed to agony—an agony so deep, it could not be expressed in words.

Suddenly I understood the significance of what I was hearing. It was none other than the voice of Satan himself as he was compelled to give up his throne in heaven and to take up a new abode on the level of earth.

Scripture indicates that up to the present time Satan and his angels have retained a position in heaven. It will only be as a result of the future conflict described above that they will finally be evicted from the heavenlies and cast down to the earth.

But this will not be a conflict only of angels. The believers on earth will also have their part to play: "And they [the believers on earth] overcame him [Satan] by the blood of the Lamb and by the word of their testimony, and they did not love their lives to the death" (verse 11).

It is important for us to recognize that the victory in this conflict against Satan's kingdom will only come through a joint action by God's angels in heaven and the believers on earth. This challenges us to ask whether or not we on earth are sensitive to what is taking place in heaven and ready to play our part.

Could it be said of us as Christians on earth: "They did not love their lives to the death"? This describes *total commitment*. Picture yourself confronted by a situation in which you have only two alternatives: *to lay down your life or to renege on your testimony to Jesus*. Which would you choose? For the kind of believers described in Revelation 12:11, it is more important to do the will of Jesus than to hold on to life.

The comment that follows this account of Satan being cast out of heaven indicates that it will take place close to the end of the present dispensation.

"Therefore rejoice, O heavens, and you who dwell in them! Woe to the inhabitants of the earth and the sea! For the devil has come down to you, having great wrath, because he knows that he has a short time."

verse 12

Some people reading this account of Satan being cast out of heaven have assumed that the events described must have followed immediately after Christ's death and resurrection. According to the description given here, however, this cannot be true, because at this point the devil knows *he has but a short time.* Two thousand years have elapsed since the death and resurrection of Jesus. This could not be described as a "short time."

To the contrary, the description of these events given here indicates that they will occur very near to the close of the present dispensation, not to its opening two thousand years ago.

Of all our conflicts with Satan, this is likely to prove the fiercest and most exacting. At this point he will recognize that his time is short. At its conclusion he is fully aware that he will be confined in the bottomless pit, as described in Revelation 20:1–3:

> Then I saw an angel coming down from heaven, having the key to the bottomless pit and a great chain in his hand. He laid hold of the dragon, that serpent of old, who is the Devil and Satan, and bound him for a thousand years; and he cast him into the bottomless pit, and shut him up.

Even the bottomless pit, however, is not Satan's final destination. Beyond this, his ultimate and eternal destiny is finally disclosed in verse 10 of the same chapter:

> The devil, who deceived them, was cast into the *lake of fire* and brimstone where the beast and the false prophet are. And they will be tormented day and night forever and ever.
>
> emphasis added

There is one further extremely important fact contained in Revelation 12:11. It reveals the weapons by which the believers on earth achieve victory: *the blood of the Lamb and the word of their testimony*. The Lamb, of course, is "the Lamb of God who takes away the sin of the world"—the Lord Jesus Christ (John 1:29).

It is the blood of Jesus that gives us the victory—but only as we learn to testify about it. It is our testimony that releases its power. This places a clear, practical responsibility on all of us: *As believers, we must testify personally to what the Word says that the blood of Jesus does for us.*

> It is the blood of Jesus that gives us the victory—but only as we learn to testify about it.

Perhaps the greatest single picture in the Old Testament of the blood of Christ and its power is the sacrifice of the Passover lamb instituted for the Israelites while they were in Egypt. God made every Israelite father responsible to select and kill a lamb and to apply its blood to his home. This is how it was to be done:

> "Now you shall keep it [the lamb] until the fourteenth day of the same month. Then the whole assembly of the congregation of Israel shall kill it at twilight. And they shall take some of the blood and put it on the two doorposts and on the lintel of the houses where they eat it."
>
> Exodus 12:6–7

In the following verses, God explains to the people of Israel why this is necessary:

> "For I will pass through the land of Egypt on that night, and will strike all the firstborn in the land of Egypt, both man and beast; and against all the gods of Egypt I will execute judgment: I am the LORD. Now the blood shall be

a sign for you on the houses where you are. And when I see the blood, I will pass over you; and the plague shall not be on you to destroy you when I strike the land of Egypt."

verses 12–13

God gave exact details of how the blood was to be applied. It is obvious that if you simply kill a lamb out in the open, its blood will pour out upon the ground and not be preserved for any special purpose. Scripture makes it clear that when the Passover lamb was killed, its blood was to be caught carefully in a basin so that it could be appropriately applied:

> Then Moses called for all the elders of Israel and said to them, "Pick out and take lambs for yourselves according to your families, and kill the Passover lamb. And you shall take a bunch of hyssop, dip it in the blood that is in the basin, and strike the lintel and the two doorposts with the blood that is in the basin. And none of you shall go out of the door of his house until morning."

verses 21–22

The protection for Israel was only through the blood of the lamb. They were not saved because they were Israelites; natural descent from Abraham did not protect them. The only thing that protected them was meeting God's requirements with the blood of the lamb.

When the lamb was killed and its blood was caught in a basin, then the sacrifice was complete, and the blood was available. However, as long as the blood remained in the basin it did not protect a single Israelite family. They could all have killed a lamb and caught the blood but left it in the basin. The same judgment that came upon the Egyptians would have come upon them.

God required the Israelites to transfer the blood from the basin to the most conspicuous place in every Israelite home: the front door. It had to be applied to the door—to the lintel and to both side posts on the outside where it could be plainly visible to anyone who passed by.

There was, however, one place to which the blood was never applied: the threshold. No Israelite was ever permitted to trample on that sacred blood.

God said, "When I see the blood upon the lintel and on the doorposts, then *I will pass over you* and I will not allow the destroyer to enter into you" (see verse 23). That is why the ceremony is called "Passover."

Only when the blood was transferred from the basin to the door did it protect the Israelite family that lived inside that house. All this depicts what is made available to us through the sacrifice of Jesus, who in 1 Corinthians 5:7 is actually called "our Passover": "For indeed Christ, our Passover, was sacrificed for us."

Jesus as the Lamb of God is here identified with the Passover lamb that was killed in Egypt. The point that needs to be emphasized and that is of vital personal importance for each of us is that the Lamb—Jesus—has already been sacrificed. His blood has already been shed. To carry the analogy through from the Old Testament to the New Testament, the blood in the basin depicts Jesus' blood already shed for us.

But just as the blood in the basin protected no Israelite in Egypt, the fact that Christ has died and shed His blood on the cross protects no one now. There are no benefits to any of us merely because of the fact that Christ died and shed His blood. In the land of Egypt, the Israelites had to *transfer* the blood from the basin to their own homes, their own situations, the places where they lived, the places of need. Only when the blood was transferred and applied in this way did it become effective.

The same principle applies to you and me. We believe in Jesus Christ, we believe He is the Lamb of God, we believe His blood has been shed and that everything we need—full salvation—is available through His blood. But as long as the blood remains "in the basin," it does not do any of us any good. It is a potential blessing, but until it is effectively applied, it achieves nothing positive.

We have seen that under the Old Covenant God gave Israel only one means to transfer the blood to the place where it was needed: a bunch of hyssop. There is nothing beautiful or romantic about hyssop. It grows almost everywhere in the Middle East and is as readily available to the poor as to the rich. The Israelites had to pluck the hyssop, dip it in the blood in the basin and then strike it against the door—the lintel and the doorposts of their homes. In this way, the blood was transferred from the basin to the home.

In the New Covenant, we do not use hyssop. But God has given us something that corresponds to the hyssop. What makes the blood available and effective in our lives, in our situations? The answer is found in Revelation 12:11: "And they overcame him [the accuser] by the blood of the Lamb and by the word of their *testimony*" (emphasis added).

When I testify about the blood, I am applying it to my situation. My testifying about the blood in the New Covenant is exactly analogous to the Israeli father in the Old

Covenant dipping the hyssop in the basin and striking it on the doorposts of his home. When the blood was applied in this way, its protection was perfect.

So it is with you and me. There is total, perfect protection in the blood of the Lamb, the Lord Jesus Christ. But it protects none of us until it is applied. Until we learn to testify personally to what the Word of God says that the blood of Jesus does for us, we have no benefits from the blood. All our believing does not change anything until we combine it with our personal testimony.

> There is total, perfect protection in the blood of the Lamb, the Lord Jesus Christ.

The moment we begin to testify, however, Satan will turn loose everything he has to frighten us, to make us feel shy, embarrassed and ashamed. He will do anything he can to prevent us from coming out with a clear, bold, scriptural testimony to the blood of Jesus. But when we do testify, we take hold of a weapon against which Satan has no defense. The Passover blood repelled the destroyer and he was not allowed any access to the family sheltered behind it. The blood of Jesus is just as effective for us today.

But remember just one important fact about the believers described in Revelation 12:11: "They did not love their lives to the death." Would that be true of you and me?

Revelation 12:10 depicts the victory that is waiting for us as believers:

> Then I heard a loud voice saying in heaven, "Now salvation, and strength, and the kingdom of our God, and the

power of His Christ have come, for the accuser of our brethren, who accused them before our God day and night, has been cast down."

All heaven is waiting for us to win this victory. Salvation is already provided for us by Jesus. But it does not come experientially until we have made it work in our lives. Only then does heaven respond and say, "*Now* has come salvation."

> Jesus won the victory for us at Calvary, but salvation has not yet come to us personally until we have fulfilled the scriptural conditions and applied His victory in our own lives.

The same is true in the life of the individual believer. Jesus won the victory for us at Calvary, but salvation has not yet come to us personally until we have fulfilled the scriptural conditions and applied His victory in our own lives.

This is true both for God's people collectively and for each of us as individuals. Salvation has not come until the power of the blood of Jesus has actually been released to do its work in us. Only then can we truly say, "*Now* salvation has come."

If we are to overcome Satan by testifying personally to what the Word says the blood does for us, one essential requirement is that we must *know* what the Word says about the blood. Otherwise, we have no testimony.

This will be the theme of our next chapter.

Questions for This Study

1. Two of Satan's tactics in dealing with Christians are
   _____ and _____.

2. What is the only way to victory in the conflict against
   Satan's kingdom?

   _____

   _____

3. What is one way you could describe not loving your
   life to the death?

   _____

   _____

4. When did the blood become effective for the Israelites
   in Egypt, and when does the blood of Jesus become
   effective for a believer today?

   (a) _____

   _____

   (b) _____

   _____

   _____

Life Application

1. Take this opportunity to apply the knowledge of what
   you have just learned. Apply the blood of Jesus to
   your life and the situations you are experiencing.

2. What are the benefits of testifying about the faithful-
   ness of God?

Notes

_____

_____

_____

_____

_____

_____

Memory Verse

For though we walk in the flesh, we do not war according to the flesh. For the weapons of our warfare are not carnal but mighty in God for pulling down strongholds, casting down arguments and every high thing that exalts itself against the knowledge of God, bringing every thought into captivity to the obedience of Christ.

2 Corinthians 10:3–5

Faith Response

Father, thank You for sending me the perfect, spotless Lamb, Jesus Christ, sacrificed for me. By His blood I have been forgiven, cleansed and set free from sin and all its effects. I know that my future is with You because of Him. Thank You, Lord Jesus, for coming for me, for taking my place, for paying for my sin and for giving me new life. Let me apply Your victory to my own life, and not love my life to the death.

By the Blood of the Lamb

When I came to understand how vital it is to maintain a consistent personal testimony about the blood of Jesus, I was motivated to search through the Scriptures and see what this required of me. I am going to share with you five passages that I have found especially effective.

Redemption

The first Scripture is Ephesians 1:7: "In Him [Christ] we have redemption through His blood, the forgiveness of sins, according to the riches of His grace."

First of all, to receive these benefits we must be *in Christ*. This means coming to the end of ourselves and making an unreserved commitment to Jesus. Then when we are in Christ, we have redemption through His blood. *To redeem* means "to buy back, to pay a ransom price." We were in the hands of the devil; we were Satan's slaves. But on the cross Jesus paid the ransom price of His blood to buy us back to God.

This is confirmed also in 1 Peter 1:18–19:

> . . . knowing that you were not redeemed with corruptible things, like silver or gold, from your aimless conduct received by tradition from your fathers, but with the precious blood of Christ, as of a lamb without blemish and without spot.

Before we came to Christ, we followed an ungodly way of living, even though we may have practiced religious customs. We were in the grip of Satan, we were under condemnation because of our sins and we were open to the attacks of the devourer and the destroyer.

But we were bought back! How? Only by the precious blood of Jesus Christ as the sacrificial Lamb of God. He was without blemish, that is without original sin, and without spot, that is without personal sin. He was the sinless Lamb of God upon whom the sins of the world were laid. It is only through His blood that we are redeemed. No other price could pay for our redemption.

How then does God expect us to respond? "Let the redeemed of the LORD *say so,* whom He has redeemed from the hand of the enemy" (Psalm 107:2, emphasis added).

God expects us to make a bold declaration. We are to *say* that we have been redeemed. This Scripture also clarifies from whom we have been redeemed. We have been redeemed from the hand of the enemy. Who is the enemy?

According to Scripture, the devil is our adversary. We were in the hand of the devil, but we were bought out of his hand by the blood of Jesus.

What is our testimony, then, in the light of Ephesians 1:7 and Psalm 107:2?

Through the blood of Jesus, I am redeemed out of the hand of the devil.

The more you confess this, the more effective it becomes in your life! Making this confession is the same as striking the blood on the doorposts of your heart.

Forgiveness of Sins

Ephesians 1:7 makes a second statement about the blood: "In Him [Christ] we have . . . the forgiveness of sins, according to the riches of His grace."

Another thing purchased for us, therefore, by the blood of Jesus is the forgiveness of our sins. This agrees with what Jesus said at the Last Supper as He gave His disciples the cup, which was the emblem of His blood: "For this is My blood of the new covenant, which is shed for many for the remission [forgiveness] of sins" (Matthew 26:28).

In Hebrews 9:22 this is confirmed: "And according to the law almost all things are purified with blood, and without shedding of blood there is no remission [forgiveness]."

The blood of Jesus was shed that our sins might be forgiven. In Ephesians 1:7, Paul makes these two things coextensive:

Redemption through the blood of Jesus.
The forgiveness of sins.

Thus, it is very important to understand that we have the full legal rights of redemption only insofar as our sins are forgiven. If all our sins are forgiven, we have the total rights of redemption. But if we have unconfessed or unforgiven sin in our lives, in that area we do not have the full legal rights of redemption. Satan still has a claim in that area.

I have proved this many times when ministering to those who need deliverance from evil spirits. If Satan has a legitimate claim against a person, he will not give it up. You can shout in his face, you can fast for a week, you can summon the most anointed preacher, you can do whatever you like, but it will not change the devil because he knows that he has a legal claim in that area.

I want to mention another common way in which believers give Satan a legal claim in their own lives: their failure to forgive others. After teaching His disciples the Lord's Prayer, Jesus follows up with this warning:

> "For if you forgive men their trespasses, your heavenly Father will also forgive you. But if you do not forgive men their trespasses, neither will your Father forgive your trespasses."

> Matthew 6:14–15

We are not entitled to claim forgiveness from God above the measure in which we forgive others. Therefore, if there is any person whom we have not totally forgiven, in that measure, correspondingly, we are not forgiven of God.

That area of unforgiveness in our lives is one in which Satan still has a legal claim. We cannot dislodge him until we have canceled his claim by forgiving the person or persons whom we need to forgive.

Remember, redemption is coextensive with the forgiveness of our sins. If all our sins are forgiven, then we have the total rights of redemption. Satan has no legal claim outstanding against us. But if sin has not been dealt with in some area in our lives, Satan still has a legal claim in that area. No matter how anointed the minister may be whom we ask to pray for us, the devil will not be dislodged because he knows he has a legal right to occupy that territory. The devil is a legal expert. It is essential, therefore, that we know God's conditions for total forgiveness, and that we have met them.

> If all our sins are forgiven, we have the total rights of redemption. But if we have unconfessed or unforgiven sin in our lives, in that area we do not have the full legal rights of redemption. Satan still has a claim in that area.

To sum up our text in Ephesians 1:7, this leads us to two conclusions: One, we must be willing to confess and renounce all of our sins; and, two, we must be willing to forgive totally all persons who have ever trespassed against us, harmed us or wronged us.

Then and only then can our second testimony be: *Through the blood of Jesus, all my sins are forgiven.*

Cleansing

The third statement about the blood is found in 1 John 1:7: "But if we walk in the light as He is in the light, we have fellowship with one another, and the blood of Jesus Christ His Son cleanses us from all sin."

This passage reveals three things that are bound together in the Word of God and that cannot be separated. These are:

Walking in the light.
Fellowship one with another.
Cleansing by the blood of Jesus.

I have dealt with scores of people who claimed the cleansing and protection of the blood, but who did not lead the kind of life that entitled them to receive it. According to this verse, the blood of Jesus Christ cleansing us is a consequence that follows after we have met a condition introduced by the word *if*: "*If* we are walking in the light." Then two results follow: First, we have fellowship one with another and, second, the blood of Jesus cleanses us from all sin.

Certain logical conclusions follow: If we are not walking in fellowship with our fellow believers, that is evidence that we are not walking in the light. And if we are not walking in the light, again, logically, it follows that we cannot claim the cleansing of the blood of Jesus. So we come to this conclusion: If we are out of fellowship, we are out of the light. And if we are out of the light, the blood no longer cleanses us. The blood of Jesus cleanses only in the light.

Unfortunately, many Christians deceive themselves about their right of access to the blood. They keep quoting the latter part of 1 John 1:7, but in many cases they have never fulfilled the condition preceded by "if": *walking in the light as He is in the light.*

Thus, the evidence that we are walking in the light is that we are in fellowship one with another: Out of fellowship, out of the light. Out of the light, no longer under the cleansing of the blood of Jesus.

Fellowship is two-directional. First, with God and, second, with our fellow believers. This makes fellowship with God, and with one another, of unique significance in our lives. The closer our fellowship, the brighter the light. As we mature in Christ, we come to a place where there are no longer any shadows, no dark corners, nothing swept under the rug, nothing covered up. That is a very frightening place for the natural man! It is a place of *transparency.* But that is the only place where the blood of Jesus completely fulfills its function of cleansing. To claim the cleansing of the blood of Jesus without fulfilling these prior conditions is to make the blood cheap, and the blood of Jesus is not cheap. It is the most precious thing in the universe.

> As we mature in Christ, we come to a place where there are no longer any shadows, no dark corners, nothing swept under the rug, nothing covered up.

My dear brother or sister, you have no alternative but to come to the light. What does it mean to come to the light? Confess your sins, first to God and then to any person against whom you have sinned. Bring everything out into the open.

Is that a difficult thing for people to do? The answer is yes! The light seems so bright. We tend to recoil from it, saying: *I could never bring that terrible thing out into the open—that awful memory, that guilty secret, that enslaving habit—I could not expose it to the light.* The natural man shrinks from it. But the wonderful secret is this: When your sin is exposed to the light, the blood of Jesus washes it away and everything is clean.

God actually says this in Jeremiah 31:34: "I will forgive their iniquity, and their sin I will remember no more."

God does not have a bad memory, but He does have a supernatural "eraser" that blots out the memory of sin once it has been forgiven.

On the other hand, if you do not bring your sin into the light, your sin remains. Consider once again this tremendous principle: *The blood of Jesus cleanses only in the light.*

Suppose that we have met the conditions: We are walking in the light, and we are in fellowship with our fellow believers. Then we have the right to make this testimony:

The blood of Jesus Christ, God's Son, is cleansing me, now and continually, from all sin.

It is very important to see that this is a continuing present tense. The blood cleanses continually as we walk continually in the light. They are two ongoing operations. Continuing to walk in the light, we continue to receive the cleansing of the blood. This is the total cleansing work of the blood.

Justification

The fourth statement about the blood is made in Romans 5:8–9:

> But God demonstrates His own love toward us, in that while we were still sinners, Christ died for us. Much more then, having now been justified by His blood, we shall be saved from wrath through Him.

Our proclamation is taken from the middle phrase of Romans 5:9: "We are justified by the blood of Jesus." *Justified* is one of those religious words that people often use but do not understand; other people are scared by it. Think about it this way: Wherever you read in the King James Version the word *just,* you can substitute the word *righteous.* That is true both in the Hebrew of the Old Testament and in the Greek of the New Testament. In each language, there is one word that the King James translators alternately translate *righteous* or *just.* When it is a matter of legal processes, they tend to use the word *just.* But when it is a matter of practical living, they tend to use the word *righteous.* Whichever translation is used, in the original language it is one and the same word.

The problem with the use of the word *justified* is that people tend to reserve it for a kind of formal transaction in a legal atmosphere. Somewhere up in the remote courts of heaven, they reason, *something happened* and now everything is all right. But this is expressing only half the meaning of the word. *To be justified* means "to be made just or righteous." I prefer the word *righteous* because it brings it right down to where I live—my home, my business, my personal relationships. *Just* sounds as if it is describing a legal formality that has to be transacted in some remote court somewhere and does not have much application to my life. But *righteous* immediately brings it down to daily life.

The Scripture says we have been *made righteous* by the blood of Jesus. You are not justified if you have not been made righteous in your daily living. It is more than a legal ceremony; it is more than a change of labels. It is a radical change of character and lifestyle that is produced by the blood of Jesus.

Here is another way to understand the meaning of *justified*. You can interpret it in this way: *just-as-if-I'd* never sinned. Why? I am justified because I have been made righteous with a righteousness that is not my own, but the righteousness of Jesus Christ. This righteousness has no record of sin, no past for which it needs to be forgiven. This is now my condition before God.

Look at Romans 3:23–25:

> For all have sinned and fall short of the glory of God, being justified [made righteous] freely [without deserving it] by His grace through the redemption that is in Christ Jesus, whom God set forth as a propitiation by His blood, through faith, to demonstrate His righteousness, because in His forbearance God had passed over the sins that were previously committed.

I am grateful for the word *freely* in that verse. *Freely* means "without being earned." The problem with religious people often is that they are trying to earn righteousness and they never achieve it. The righteousness of which

Scripture speaks cannot be earned. It must be received by faith as a free gift or it cannot be received at all.

In Romans 4:4–5, Paul makes a statement that is the exact opposite of what religious people would anticipate:

> Now to him who works, the wages are not counted as grace but as debt. *But to him who does not work* but believes on Him who justifies the ungodly, his faith is accounted for righteousness.
>
> emphasis added

To receive the righteousness that God offers us through faith, the first thing we have to do is to *stop working*, stop trying to earn it. God offers to us a righteousness that we can never earn—a free gift.

The great basic truth of the Gospel is this: God makes unrighteous people righteous. Second Corinthians 5:21 says in the King James Version: "For he hath made him [Jesus] to be sin for us, who knew no sin; that we might be made the righteousness of God in him."

> The great basic truth of the Gospel is this: God makes unrighteous people righteous.

This depicts a complete exchange. Jesus was made sin with our sinfulness that we might be made righteous with His righteousness. This righteousness is available through faith in His blood and cannot be received on any other basis.

Righteousness produces certain immediate, observable results. One such result is *boldness*. This is lacking in many contemporary Christians. They are timid and apologetic and tend to back down when confronted with evil or with the devil. This is not the picture of righteousness given in Scripture: "The wicked flee when no one pursues, *but the righteous are bold as a lion*" (Proverbs 28:1, emphasis added).

The root cause of this timidity in many professing Christians is that they do not have a revelation of the fact that they are righteous in God's sight—as righteous as Jesus Christ Himself. When we receive that revelation, it makes us bold and we can then testify:

Through the blood of Jesus, I am justified, made righteous, just-as-if-I'd never sinned.

Sanctification

Now we move on to the fifth aspect of our testimony, which is sanctification. Hebrews 13:12 speaks about the *sanctifying* power of the blood of Jesus: "Therefore Jesus also, that He might sanctify the people with His own blood, suffered outside the gate."

To *sanctify* means to "make holy." Holiness includes within it the thought of "being set apart to God."

Just like righteousness, sanctification does not come by works or effort; it does not come by religion. It comes by faith in the blood of Jesus. When you are sanctified by His blood you are set apart to God.

In this connection Paul says in Colossians 1:13: "He [God] has delivered us from the power of darkness [the authority of darkness, the area of Satan's authority] and conveyed [transferred] us into the kingdom of the Son of His love."

Through faith in the blood of Jesus we have been removed from the area of Satan's authority, and transferred (translated) into the Kingdom of God and of Jesus Christ.

The word *conveyed* means to "carry over from one place to another place." In Scripture, it describes a total and complete transfer. In the Old Testament two men were translated (conveyed) from earth to heaven, Enoch and Elijah. Both of them went in their entirety. The only thing that Elijah left behind was his mantle, but his body went with him.

This is what I understand Paul's words to mean: *We have been totally transferred from the kingdom of darkness to the Kingdom of God's marvelous light!* The Scripture does not say that we *are going* to be transferred, it says that we *have been* transferred—spirit, soul and body. We are no longer in the devil's territory; we are not under the devil's laws. We are in the Kingdom of the Son of God, and we are under His laws.

Romans 8:2 further defines these two laws: "For the law of the Spirit of life in Christ has made me free from the law of sin and death."

In this verse we see the devil's law—the law of sin and death—and we see the law of God's Kingdom—the law of the Spirit of life in Christ Jesus. Here are two kingdoms with their opposing laws in operation. Paul, speaking from his own experience, explains: "I am no longer in the devil's territory, I am not under the devil's law. His kingdom does not apply to me because I have been transferred to another kingdom. I have been translated—carried over, spirit, soul and body."

Therefore, our fifth testimony is:

Through the blood of Jesus I am sanctified, made holy, set apart to God.

Here then are the five testimonies that each of us may make about the blood of Jesus:

Through the blood of Jesus, I am redeemed out of the hand of the devil.

Through the blood of Jesus, all my sins are forgiven.

The blood of Jesus Christ, God's Son, is cleansing me, now and continually, from all sin.

Through the blood of Jesus, I am justified, made righteous, just-as-if-I'd never sinned.

Through the blood of Jesus I am sanctified, made holy, set apart to God.

When we testify to the blood of Jesus, the Holy Spirit bears witness to His work of redemption in our lives. It is our testifying that releases the operation of the blood in our lives. If we do not testify, nothing goes into operation. It is our personal testimony that triggers Satan's defeat. This helps us to understand why we so often experience opposition when we begin to testify. It is at this point that we are really beginning to do the devil some harm. We can believe anything we like and the devil is not too disturbed until we start to testify about it. But when we start to testify, then he is going to do everything he can

> When we testify to the blood of Jesus, the Holy Spirit bears witness to His work of redemption in our lives.

to discourage us, frighten us and keep us from speaking out, because it is our testifying that makes God's power effective against him.

Questions for This Study

1. What does it mean to be "in Christ"?

_____

_____

_____

2. When is it that we have the full legal rights of redemption?

_____

_____

3. Righteousness has no _____ _____ _____
   and no _____ _____ _____ _____ _____

   _____ _____ _____.

4. What is the root cause of timidity in many Christians?

_____

_____

_____

Life Application

1. Ask the Lord to help you take inventory to see if there is anyone toward whom you have unforgiveness. If so, go before the Lord and forgive that person.

2. What does it mean to you to be righteous, and why is there a breastplate of righteousness for the heart in your armor (see Ephesians 6:14)?

Notes

_____

_____

_____

_____

_____

Memory Verse

For He made Him who knew no sin to be sin for us, that we might become the righteousness of God in Him.

2 Corinthians 5:21

Faith Response

Father, I testify to what the blood does for me:
Through the blood of Jesus, I am redeemed out of the hand of the devil.
Through the blood of Jesus, all my sins are forgiven.
Through the blood of Jesus, I am cleansed continually from all sin.
Through the blood of Jesus, I am justified, made righteous, just-as-if-I'd never sinned.

Through the blood of Jesus, I am sanctified, made holy, set apart to God.
My body is a temple of the Holy Spirit, redeemed and cleansed by the blood of Jesus.
Through the blood of Jesus, Satan has no place in me and no power over me.

12 What Kind of People?

In the previous chapter, I listed five scriptural proclamations concerning the blood of Jesus. I said that making and maintaining these scriptural proclamations is the key to a life of victory over sin and Satan. I could easily imagine that some would respond: Is it really that simple? Is that all we have to do?

My reply is this: The key to success does not depend solely on what we *say* but on what we *are*. You will recall that in Revelation 12:11, the people who achieved this victory over sin and Satan are described as follows: "They did not love their lives to the death."

How are we to understand that? I have looked in various translations of the Bible but I have not found anything that to my mind describes satisfactorily the kind of people referred to. What does it mean, "They did not love their lives to the death"?

Here is my own interpretation of this phrase. I suggest

187

that for these people it was more important to do the will of God than to stay alive. Confronted by a situation in which to do the will of God would cost them their lives, that is the price they would pay. They would not look for any alternative, any way out.

The word I would use to describe such people is *committed*. Such people are committed to obeying the Word of God and to doing the will of God regardless of the consequences for their own lives.

Luke 9:21–24 pictures an enthusiastic crowd following Jesus, excited by the miracles they have witnessed. But apparently Jesus is more interested in personal commitment than in that kind of enthusiasm:

> Then He said to them all, "If anyone desires to come after Me, let him deny himself, and take up his cross daily, and follow Me. For whoever desires to save his life will lose it, but whoever loses his life for My sake will save it."
>
> Luke 9:23–24

The message of Jesus does not promise an easy way through life. On the contrary, in the Sermon on the Mount, He exhorts:

> "Enter by the narrow gate; for *wide is* the gate and *broad is* the way that leads to destruction, and there are many who go in by it. Because *narrow is* the gate and *difficult is* the way which leads to life, and there are few who find it."
>
> Matthew 7:13–14, emphasis added

If your picture of the Christian life does not include God's demands for sacrifice and a life laid down, you may need to question the "way" that you are traveling on. You may discover that you are on the broad, easy way that leads to destruction and not on the narrow, difficult way that leads to life. In the contemporary church some ministries emphasize only the blessings and benefits of the Christian life and never speak about the conditions that we have to fulfill in order to obtain those blessings and benefits. Such ministries could be compared to a merchant who displays an attractive range of goods, but never attaches a price tag to any of them.

> If your picture of the Christian life does not include God's demands for sacrifice and a life laid down, you may need to question the "way" that you are traveling on.

I have often been blessed—and challenged—by Luke's account of Paul's journey to Rome given in Acts 27 and 28. This was no casual trip; it was a vital, strategic move in the purposes of God. According to Galatians 2:7, God had committed to Paul the responsibility of bringing the Gospel to the "uncircumcised"—i.e., the whole Gentile world. The key to this would be to establish a center in the city of Rome. From there, many different channels would automatically carry the Gospel to the whole ancient world—channels of commerce, education, finance, governmental administration and natural social intercourse. Because of Paul's special calling, he was the person best qualified to establish such a center in Rome.

Because of the significance of Paul's move to Rome, he encountered tremendous spiritual opposition on his journey there. I do not know if in Paul's day there was anything corresponding to the luxury cruises that are so popular today, but I do know that Paul was not on such a cruise. On the contrary, he was traveling on a freight ship as a prisoner in chains. Furthermore, the ship was caught up in a storm so horrific that for two full weeks the people on board never caught a glimpse of the sun by day or of the moon and the stars by night.

Let me mention that a storm of such intensity was generated by more than natural forces. There are examples of this in the Old Testament. Job 1:19, for example, records a supernatural storm directed by Satan against Job's sons and daughters. A messenger came to Job with the following report:

> "Suddenly a great wind came from across the wilderness and struck the four corners of the house, and it fell on the young people, and they are dead; and I alone have escaped to tell you!"

On the basis of many years in Christian ministry, I would say that any wind that can strike all four corners of a dwelling simultaneously, from all directions, probably has the devil behind it.

Returning to the storm in Acts 27, we continue with Luke's narrative:

> But after long abstinence from food, then Paul stood in the midst of them and said, "Men, you should have listened to me, and not have sailed from Crete and incurred [literally, *gained*] this disaster and loss. And now I urge you to take heart, for there will be no loss of life among you, but only

of the ship. For there stood by me this night an angel of the God to whom I belong and whom I serve."

Acts 27:21–23

Paul used two phrases here to describe his relationship to God: "to whom I *belong*" and "whom I *serve*." In the economy of God's household, these two can never be separated. If we do not *belong* to God, we have no right to *serve* Him. There are no *hirelings* in God's household. On the other hand, we cannot belong to God if we are not available to Him for His service. God does not welcome to His household spoiled, self-indulgent egoists. They have no place in His Kingdom.

The Law of Moses recognized two classes of servants. Those who were paid by the day were called *hirelings*. They were not members of the household in which they were serving. Conversely, those who were members of the household did not necessarily receive any pay for their service. It was simply a natural response to the privileges they enjoyed as members of the household. But the household to which they belonged accepted responsibility for their maintenance whether at any given time they were actually working or not.

> We cannot belong to God if we are not available to Him for His service. God does not welcome to His household spoiled, self-indulgent egoists.

In His Kingdom, God has no place for hirelings. Those who serve in God's Kingdom do so because they are members of the household. This means that we cannot separate the two phrases Paul used to describe himself: "to whom I belong" and "whom I serve." Let me repeat, if we do not belong to God, we have no right to serve Him.

Eventually, the ship on which Paul and his companions were traveling was dashed against a rocky promontory and began to break up. This gave those on board an opportunity to escape to dry land.

Have you ever wondered: Was Paul in the will of God in this whole experience? As I have already indicated, I believe that Paul was fully in the will of God, and his whole journey to Rome was ordered by God. But satanic forces that feared the possible impact of Paul's ministry in Rome did everything in their power to destroy him before he could reach his destination. The storm that he encountered was not of purely natural origin but was brought about by satanic forces in the heavenlies.

In His divine wisdom, God sometimes permits His servants who are doing His will to be exposed to the malice and rage of Satan. In this way, they get insight not only into the true nature of the forces that are opposing them but also into their personal need for persistent vigilance.

In 1 Peter 5:8, the apostle warned his fellow believers: "Be sober, be vigilant; because your adversary the devil walks about like a roaring lion, seeking whom he may devour." It would be a frightening experience to encounter a hungry lion in search of prey! The Bible never instills fear into us, but, on the other hand, it never encourages us to underestimate the power and the ferocity of our satanic opponents.

After the shipwreck Satan had one more challenge. The people who had escaped safely to land began to collect fuel for a fire. Paul—the "great" apostle—did not merely stand on one side waiting for others to get their hands dirty; he was among the first to start gathering fuel. Satan used this as an opportunity to make one final attempt to destroy Paul: "A viper came out [of the bundle of sticks] because of the heat, and fastened on his [Paul's] hand" (Acts 28:3–5). Out of all 276 people, why did the viper choose Paul as its victim? Was there some supernatural intelligence operating through that viper?

But Paul was full of the Holy Spirit. He did not feel the need to pray or to speak in tongues. To the amazement of the local islanders who knew how deadly a viper's bite was, Paul simply shook the snake off into the fire and went on gathering fuel.

What was the secret of Paul's victorious life? He himself explained in 2 Timothy 1:12:

> For this reason I also suffer these things; nevertheless I am not ashamed, for I know whom I have believed and am persuaded that He is able to keep what I have *committed* to Him until that Day.
>
> emphasis added

The secret of Paul's victorious living is summed up in that one word—*committed*. He was totally at God's disposal. In Philippians 3:13–14, he stated the supreme ambition of his life:

> Brethren, I do not count myself to have apprehended; but one thing I do, forgetting those things which are behind and reaching forward to those things which are ahead, I

press toward the goal for the prize of the upward call of God in Christ Jesus.

In some sections of the contemporary church, an unscriptural separation has been introduced between salvation and holiness. Holiness is represented as being a kind of optional "add-on" to a package deal of salvation, such as tour group operators offer: "You have paid for your tour to the 'Holy Land.' For just $185 extra, you can add a visit to Egypt and a trip up the Nile."

> Achieving personal holiness is not something that God will do for us. It is something that God offers us the grace to do for ourselves.

This represents an unscriptural attitude toward holiness. In Hebrews 12:14, the writer exhorts: "Pursue peace with all people, and holiness, without which no one will see the Lord." Holiness is not an optional "add-on" to the package deal of salvation. On the contrary, without holiness, no one will see the Lord.

In 2 Corinthians 7:1, Paul appealed to his fellow believers to join him in the pursuit of personal holiness: "Therefore, having these promises, beloved, let us cleanse ourselves from all filthiness of the flesh and spirit, *perfecting holiness* in the fear of God" (emphasis added). Achieving personal holiness is not something that God will do for us. It is something that God offers us the grace to do for ourselves. It cannot be separated from the fear of God. It is the logical outworking of our personal commitment to Jesus and an essential condition of the victory over Satan that God has promised us.

The last two verses of Acts give a wonderful picture of the victory that concluded Paul's tempestuous journey:

> Then Paul dwelt two whole years in his own rented house, and received all who came to him, preaching the kingdom of God and teaching the things which concern the Lord Jesus Christ with all confidence, no one forbidding him.

An appropriate comment would surely be: "Mission accomplished!" The Gospel for the Gentiles had been established in the city that dominated the whole Gentile world—Rome!

But there is also a personal application that we can make in our own lives. Think back for a moment about the believers described in Revelation 12:11 who "did not love their lives to the death." We each need to ask ourselves: Does this describe me?

If you cannot respond with a confident yes to this question, the Holy Spirit may be inviting you right now to make an unreserved, personal commitment to the Lord Jesus. You can say:

Lord Jesus, I thank You that on the cross You gave Yourself for me. In response, I now give myself unreservedly to You, to live my life in Your service and for Your glory. Amen!

Questions for This Study

1. The key to success does not depend solely on what we _____ but on what we _____.

2. The picture of the Christian life should include God's demands for _____ and a _____ _____ _____.

3. What are the two types of servants and their positions?

   (a) _____

   _____

   _____

   _____

   (b) _____

   _____

   _____

   _____

4. How does Derek describe the goal of achieving personal holiness?

   _____

   _____

   _____

   _____

   _____

Life Application

1. What does it mean to you to love not your life to the death, and what is your commitment to this?

2. How has this book helped you understand and participate in spiritual warfare?

Notes

_____

_____

_____

_____

_____

Memory Verse

Brethren, I do not count myself to have apprehended; but one thing I do, forgetting those things which are behind and reaching forward to those things which are ahead, I press toward the goal for the prize of the upward call of God in Christ Jesus.

Philippians 3:13–14

Faith Response

Father, I recommit my life to You and Your Kingdom. I trust You to watch over and provide for me. I know that You are always faithful and that Your plans for me are always good. Together we will accomplish what You have for me to do. I will endeavor to do my part so that when I stand before You, I will hear You say, "Well done, good and faithful servant."

Appendix

Here are the five testimonies to the blood of Jesus:

Through the blood of Jesus, I am redeemed out of the hand of the devil.

Through the blood of Jesus, all my sins are forgiven.

The blood of Jesus Christ, God's Son, is cleansing me, now and continually, from all sin.

Through the blood of Jesus, I am justified, made righteous, just-as-if-I'd never sinned.

Through the blood of Jesus, I am sanctified, made holy, set apart to God.

Answers to Study Questions

Chapter 1: What Is Your Picture of Heaven?

1. Three heavens:
   (a) The visible heaven we can see with our eyes
   (b) The mid-heaven, an expanse with different types of beings coming and going
   (c) The location of Paradise and the place of God's personal dwelling—the most sacred place in the universe

2. Angels (messengers) / *angelos*

3. Earth / heaven

4. The three main tasks:
   (a) To be messengers for God
   (b) To be His agents sent to protect those in danger

(c) To be warriors engaged in conflict with opposing angels

Chapter 2: Life Is a Battle!

1. Three actions are accepted in the New Testament as a normal part of Christian living:
   (a) Conflict
   (b) War
   (c) Embracing the attitude of a "spiritual soldier"

2. Because he has a special calling and special responsibilities and is set apart to a special way of life

3. Radical / root problem / independence / defiant

4. A deep, settled, abiding inward peace

Chapter 3: A Pre-Adamic World

1. The various words and meanings used for *tohu* and *bohu* given throughout this chapter:
   Tohu: confusion; without form; wasteland; wilderness
   Bohu: emptiness; void

2. Heaven / Lucifer

3. Revelation given us as members of the Adamic race to tell us things we need to know for our spiritual benefit

4. Do not understand / areas of truth / clear understanding

Chapter 4: Lucifer Challenges God

1. To undermine the various forms of authority God has established, both in the Church and in the world

2. Pride

3. Lucifer was not in the form of God; he was a created being. Even so, he grasped at equality with God, and in so doing fell. Jesus, by contrast, was by eternal nature divine. Even so, He did not grasp equality with God; rather, He humbled himself.

4. Self-humbling

Chapter 5: The Adamic Race: Our Origin

1. Restore you, renew you, and ultimately bring forth out of you something completely new

2. They begin to see things—and themselves—as they really are. From that point on, God continues to work in their lives in the light.

3. Something in mankind that uniquely corresponds to something in God

4. Right decision / Gospel / appropriate lifestyle / salvation

Chapter 6: The Adamic Race: Our Destiny

1. Ruler / have dominion / all

2. God's Word. Our attitude toward it determines our attitude toward God. The place God's Word has in our lives is the place God Himself has. The same honor and respect we owe to God, we owe to His Word.

3. By how you respond to God's Word

4. "All things that pertain to life and godliness" through the knowledge of Christ and the "exceedingly great and precious promises" of His Word

Chapter 7: One Man and His Prayer

1. Earthly kingdoms / empires / governments

2. They underestimate their own influence and potential

3. Authority / power

4. That effective praying tests our character and demands single-hearted commitment

Chapter 8: Angelic Beings

1. God Himself

2. Flame of fire / "Man"

3. Ministering spirits (or servant messengers)

4. Bring revelations; deliver other messages; serve the saints on earth; provide protection; intervene politically; rescue in time of need

Chapter 9: Angels at War

1. The authority God has committed to them over a certain territory

2. To release the authority of God's Word into a situation

3. The three forms of spiritual warfare that God's people and His angels are called to use:
   (a) Make proclamations
   (b) Praise
   (c) Worship

4. Two examples of angels (either of God or of Satan) with positions of specific oversight:
   (a) Michael, the archangel over the people of Israel
   (b) The prince of Persia, the satanic angel enforcing Satan's purposes in that land

Chapter 10: Now Salvation Has Come!

1. Division / guilt

2. Joint action by God's angels in heaven and believers on earth

3. Total commitment—recognizing that doing the will of Jesus is more important than holding on to life

4. The blood becomes effective:

(a) For the Israelites in Egypt when it was transferred with hyssop from a basin to their doorposts and lintels

(b) When a believer today testifies about what the blood of Jesus does for him or her

Chapter 11: By the Blood of the Lamb

1. Coming to the end of ourselves and making an unreserved commitment to Jesus

2. When all our sins are forgiven

3. Record of sin / past for which it needs to be forgiven

4. No revelation of the fact that they are righteous in God's sight—as righteous as Jesus Christ Himself

Chapter 12: What Kind of People?

1. Say / are

2. Sacrifice / life laid down

3. The two types of servants and their positions:

(a) Hirelings, paid by the day, not members of the household they are serving

(b) Servants, not necessarily paid for their service, since it is a natural response to the privileges they enjoy as members of the household (which accepts responsibility for their maintenance, whether or not they are actually working at any given time)

4. It is not something God does for us. It is something He offers us—the grace to do for ourselves. It cannot be separated from the fear of God, but is the logical outworking of our personal commitment to Jesus. It is an essential condition of the victory over Satan that God has promised us.

Subject Index

Subject Index

Scripture Index

Genesis

1:1 44, 48–49, 51, 58, 78
1:2 44, 48, 52, 56, 57, 58, 79, 81
1:3 80, 81
1:26 82, 89, 91, 97
1:26–27 78
1:27 84
2:7 52, 80, 84, 85
2:16–17 105
2:19–20 99
2:20–24 100
2:21–24 101
2:24 83
3:1–13 44
3:2 79–80
3:4 105
3:8 104
3:14–15
3:22 83
6:2–4 111
16:9 128
16:10 128
21:18 128

Exodus

3:2 128
3:4 128
12:6–7 161
12:12–13 162
12:21–22 162
12:23 163
15:3 28–29
15:4 29
32:13 148
37:9 63

Leviticus

19:16 64

Numbers

22:31 130
22:35 130

Deuteronomy

32:10 56

Joshua

5:13–15 30

Judges

6:12–13 129
6:14 129
13:3–23 129
13:9 129
13:10 129
13:22 130

1 Samuel

2:8 136

1 Kings

8:7 131
18:42–44 120

2 Kings

19:35 131

215

Derek Prince (1915–2003) was born in India of British parents. He was educated as a scholar of Greek and Latin at Eton College and Cambridge University, England, where he held a fellowship in ancient and modern philosophy at King's College. He also studied several modern languages, including Hebrew and Aramaic, at Cambridge University and the Hebrew University in Jerusalem.

While serving with the British Army in World War II, Derek began to study the Bible and experienced a life-changing encounter with Jesus Christ. Out of that encounter he formed two conclusions: first, that Jesus Christ is alive; and second, that the Bible is a true, relevant, up-to-date book. These conclusions altered the course of his life, which he then devoted to studying and teaching the Bible.

Derek's main gift of explaining the Bible and its teaching in a clear, simple way has helped build a foundation of faith in millions of lives. His nondenominational, nonsectarian approach makes his teaching relevant and helpful to people from all racial and religious backgrounds.

He is the author of more than 50 books, and his teaching is featured on 500 audio and 160 video recordings, many of which have been translated and published in more than 60 languages. His daily radio broadcast, *Keys to Successful*

Living, is translated into Arabic, Chinese (Amoy, Cantonese, Mandarin, Shanghaiese, Swatow), Croatian, German, Malagasy, Mongolian, Russian, Samoan, Spanish and Tongan. His daily radio program continues to touch lives around the world.

For more information on Derek Prince and the many teaching resources available, please contact:

Derek Prince Ministries International
P.O. Box 19501
Charlotte, NC 28219-9501
(704) 357-3556
www.derekprince.org

More Wisdom from Derek Prince

More Wisdom from Derek Prince

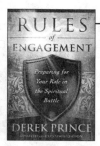
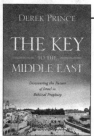